Ghost Snow Falls through the Void

(Globalization)

GHOST SNOW FALLS
THROUGH THE VOID
(Globalization)

TENNEY NATHANSON

chax 2010

ISBN 978 0925904 88 1

Chax Press
411 N 7th Ave Ste 103
Tucson, AZ 85705-8388
USA

Printed in Canada

Portions of this work have appeared in the journals *EOAGH* and *Antennae*. The author gives thanks to the editors of those journals.

Notes:

The section "Bad zen boy" borrows liberally from the "A Condolence Call: Pursuing Death into Life" chapter of John Tarrant's *Bring Me The Rhinoceros, and Other Zen Koans That Will Save Your Life*. Thanks to John for generous permission to redeploy his material.

Thanks to Joan Sutherland for generous permission to include her translations of the two Layman Pang koans that appear at the end of the book.

for my family
Lynda, Zasha, Noa, Ari
Gidette, Jake, Isaac, AnYi

Officially even a needle cannot enter,
unofficially you can drive a horse and cart through.
Linji

The poet is a counter-punching radio
Jack Spicer

This fire runs through all things.

John Tarrant

It started this way

(1.1)

In the wind, the forest inside longing,
An entryway that stillness crowded,
Sings in fear.
Sheltered things hushed.
You shriek O! Out there
Music was in change and hearing
All creatures ascended inside themselves,
brightness that built there a hut, beckoning.
Inside fear their pure beginning sings.
With a listening roar
New in darkest ear
Shelter the makeshift yet unbound silence
Of their hard lairs. O tree
Receive Orpheus from the temple where hearts nest.

*

ROCK AROUND A ROCK.

I met my sweetie
his name is Mr. Lee
he's the handsomest sweetie
that you ever did see

One two three
look at Mr. Lee
Three four five
look at him die.

Mr. Lee Mr. Lee O Mr. Lee
Mr. Lee.

*

It started this way

The near future holds a gift of contentment.
Believe it?
I remember thinking
You fall into snow time
what was it, five minutes ago?
ghost snow big and peaceful
wet and cold in your face? now you fall out of it, bump,
Today's word is kvetch. one star hung in its own void glints double through
            the pane, a warp
co-planar with the thought ghost snow falls through the void. The iterated
            snake
tessellated into its Sonoran background, tan dirt, rocks, matte colored
            foliage. The horizontal transposition topology problem
slithered like a big alert muscle—what it is! the rattle! the bottle!
that's snow right now, that is not falling in that other place,
rain drenched afternoons in the monsoon, clouds lowering beautiful and
            scary
I forgot what I was going to say
the pool, and drifting granary of airplane sky I said that
now that's snow
huge Mei-Mei-esque landscape blanketed white and flat along miles and
            miles of I-25 heading home, hushed differently through can't get
            dry & can't get wet, what's written on the stone
in the car keeping warm
& tickling under it the perpetual gentle kvetch
O P'ang "ah beautiful snow that is not falling in that other place"
what I was going to say was

item eleven
the light on the cottage porch, snow falling on the path and in the trees,
          that's no! yes!

                                                    9/11/04

*

SONG OF A ROCK (THIS IS JUST TO SAY)

I have inserted
the baton
into the asshole of
the Muslim

Forgive me
it was delicious
so sweet
and so cold

*

the Wahabi
is hot

*

freedom is
on the march!

*

we are

beheading you

*

(1.2)

transcription

song of the world
before me
desire appeared
form almost seized vanishing

wake in her now
no diaphanous distances
first meadows
felt the death--

a god singing and stepping
trees touch
where sleep
and will wander

rising perfect
in its awful heart.

*

When in doubt, let your instincts guide you.
When your instincts fail, let doubt guide you.
Today wasn't like that though? week full of rattlesnakes, road snake so
extruded I thought it was a red wire

And javelinas tinkerbelling their heft on tiny feet through the front yard
two little baby javelinas in between
today's word is prima facie I've actually never known what that meant
now I do, thanks to the javelinas? prime your face. snakes have no face
sheep have no tact said David
the falling snow has a face and it's yours
(swine before pearls, javelinas snouting the ice crystals)
Who are you? my hand reaches out through the wall of snow,
like a looming quark see here it is I hold it towards you
might mean snow haunts it as death. might not.
today's word is quantum or quandary quelled? then were we
sent here simply to ponder snow? let's A/B that
in stereo!   whooooosh!
and you: if you're an open question, please open!

9/21/04

*

he was talking
for a couple of months now

under an impulse
with which they had nothing to do.

*

News Flash Boogie

Toussaint L'ouverture
corpses floating and rotting in wash mud

lacuna
matata
extruded

banana

lament
political experiment
finito

February 9, 2005

*

(1.2.1)

rescription:

see through the world now

a god is made

no harmony that death consumes

arose—meadows, first spring

vanishing where this ear

touched form

the perfect trees.

wake her in everything

*

fortune your first choice is wisest to follow? um   well

tromping the mobius strip
sun bleeding like ink, bless the world

broom stars float the monsoon & the cattails wave in wind
flecked light the ghost snow slanting through rushes good morning my cat
        died praising the pulsing air the breeze blown death goodbye
I don't know why you say hello
ghost snow falls through the no
ratcheting light that feeds you
on the nether side shaking their white locks at the runaway sun a chorus of
        grammatical remarks
cosmically unwinds synthetic judgments getting catenary with the bobbin
        across the cosmic canyon
like girls in Busbee Berkeley wow the strip's other side's this side
completely gone, thus come, plus all of it twined
through historical consciousness   I offer the gods
this Carmen Miranda banana hat for the void
yours truly United Fruit
profane illumination
desideratum: pressed leaning out against the rough stone pediment over the
        West Side Highway, 1953? the
windshields sweeping by pristine no medial lead a smooth expanse glass
        glinting like light from the future
I was to have known myself
slammed into the oil crisis morphed into whortled digits
then unmanned drones gliding through screens over the ergonomic sands
        of Iraq
or another man's velvet reticules
"all gone now"
Baudelaire's commodity whores
fizzled into the no, no
huge afterlife of the arcades
the bursting and reforming broken glass

ghost snow falls through the now
& the tedium of fashion
is calm

the going nowhere
periplum, transnational blather
done, Don

a calm darkens among water lights
as a calm darkens among water lights Kenneth said
my periplum whortled the no
ratchet retrieval god medicine nope
the bottle!

ghosts fall through the void eating snow
where I saw the two foliages again today in the same place, flanking the
        sidewalk, soft green vegetal whomp of soap blossoms and across
        the way the shiny hard pointy ones in little redundant "pinched
        out 'ifs'"
flank of what undreamt beast
snow hisses in your ears where the huge bird caws at dawn
huddled in blankets on the screened porch, bird snow jubilato explodes new
        mantra now
glissandoed why to clam bake punctum: tiny island, tied up all night, the
        gently sloshing shore, Maine bourbon, clams clinging hard in wet
        sand squelched on up with a pop {puup!}
next day seals popping up sportifi-er than thou behind the boat exactly one
        each time
after plopping like spiders off rocks, glistening whiskers shook at the
        runaway sun's red water track, making mock
of the promise of all this
as yet unfulfilled
a dialectical image pointing
to something lost
crossing the mountains?
talkin' 'bout my generation.
hungry ghost snow falls through the void.
so I make this offering

all you demons and hungry ghosts
whose desire is never satisfied
take this food
share it with us, be at peace

decanting to: ghost snow falls through the void
eating snow.
Buddhist? historical? fried?
ping Layman P'ang now, Tenney   ring-
a-leevee-o.

spring 2005; 6/15/08

*

these uncanny phenomena placed him rather, as it happened, under the
charm

thousands of ingenuous enquirers every year, come over to see, were exactly
his sources

he had distinctly not

a more averted mind

Proportions and values were upside-down

the mere number in its long row

*

BBC News Middle East Bush Declares Victory in Iraq

landed the first sitting sailors and officers cheering
making him the ship, the 11 terror attacks
so-called tailhook
the United States never formally declared war
earlier bush sitting tailhook under interim army fry
we are pursuing and finding leaders of the old regime who will be their
        crimes
difficult work a few hundred Iraqi communists a Danish diplomat

weapons commander
announcement
was based on
an assessment.

we have begun
the search
for chemical
weapons

hundreds of killing fields know
Free nations will press on to victory

the closest the president will ever get to saying
with his helmet tucked under his arm
"of course I like it"

*

1.3
(inscription)

a mouth through the crossing
singing a god
strings our mind as you tell
opened by earth

forced: any passionate music
breath about nothing
the will, desire, stars
into shadowed voice

true lyre's real heart split
a gust inside the mouth
through the god a singing but
the voice to penetrate will end

pour a wind
that can learn to forget

*

Bad zen boy! Fritterer, snagged and sidetracked again:
"I'm not saying! I'm not saying!"
So I'm not watching snow fall down inside my body, dark and open to wind,
        right?
I'm not saying alive, I'm not saying dead.
big stretches of empty space in his music
wind cupping the snow up tossing then letting it fall, a down drift
through the coffin he banged on. Here's the daily report:
big cottonwoods hopped up suddenly in the hot wind
the palm tree clattering shaking loose its birds, skeining away toward the
        mountain like gum

the water below it clear, palm fronds adrift. because you can look all the way
        through it right down to the bottom
today's word is ersatz. there's no such thing! flock, snow piled in drifts,
        blossoms slanting down
to pound on the coffin like snow. No? I'm just saying.
plus I'm liking Frost's poem about the well
and this other poem by Frost I wrote it:

     Frost

       These must not think on to his dark bells
       Wind and the frozen lake.
       Think of sound's sleep and the evening
       Silences, snow and lovely, darkest miles.

Right now I don't like it. I like
I'm not saying alive, I'm not saying dead
a gust inside the mouth for sure, and head
it's a very quiet gust
through which you can listen to all the dust settle there
inside your head, and upper arms apparently
which is pretty strange but no stranger
than the man in his open coffin, the poor monk smashing the lid
or Richie   because the river done brought you home
as snow, falling through the coffin singing praises of falling snow caught in
        updrafts blowing slanted right out of the canvas
leaving ghost snow

which is not falling in that other place?

I'll ask my Chihuahua, & we'll get back to you

on that.

                                    8/1/05

*

whom you might meet and feel
the impulse to watch or follow

thrilled and flushed with it—
very much

windows

of them

*

I hate to be the bearer of good news
Best of all, the poorer nations are leading the way.
What explains all this good news?
The short answer is this thing
we call globalization
bad government and AIDS, sub-Saharan Africa
produces losers. lower trade barriers, shore up property rights, trade
is surging. The poor nations that opened
should be cheering on those guys in pin-stripe suits
jetting around the world Thanks
in part, to them

*

google uganda chocolate child slave labor

Our journey had advanced --

     Toil of Children: The Use of Child Labor in American ...
     Chocolate Consumption in the United States. . . .

Our feet were almost come

google is down?

To that odd Fork in Being's Road --
... Labor Department report on slavery in Uganda and Tanzania ...

Eternity -- by Term --

Our pace took sudden awe --

Our feet -- reluctant -- led --
Before -- were Cities -

to prevent use of child slaves on plantations producing cocoa for chocolate
        candies ...

                -- but Between --
The US Chocolate Manufacturers Association
The Forest of the Dead -

vowed to fight the Engel amendment tooth
Retreat -- was out of Hope --
Behind -- a Sealed Route --
and nail.

Eternity's White Flag -- Before --

The Chocolate Manufacturers Association offered to work with international
organisations, local governments and human rights organisations "to
support the Ivorian government's efforts to end child trafficking." As an
industry,

cherubic? yeah,

cherubic!

we strongly condemn abusive labour practices, and our goal is to be part of
the worldwide effort to solve this problem. If one child is affected, that is
one child

a   glinting   sword   ?

too many. The US House of Representatives recently moved to curtail use
of child slave labour on African cocoa plantations by passing a measure that
would require US food companies to certify that no part of their product was
made by workers held against their will.
approved by a vote of 291-115

And God -- at every Gate --

"We should ensure that all Americans, particularly children, who eat
chocolate, can do so with the knowledge that no children were forced into
slave labour to make their candy bar or treat,"

August 29, 2005

   *

FORTUNE
early morning news roundup:
colder than a witch's tit!
cold enough to freeze the balls off a brass monkey!
now (later) the gambol quail mill about companionably pecking seeds in
       the warmer light, doing their German burgher bird thing, boing.
       Second Breakfast in *Buddenbrooks* yum
till the town's high medieval walls vised in on him like a wedged head driving
       him blind
to which the crests say boing

the mind is an enigma, nope
O you to whom apostrophe is forbidden
as a matter of tact
may your morning class go well, your nose not drip too much
now I sound my barbaric yawp over the roofs of the world thanks Mary
Montoya in New Mexico understanding that for me
that's not right—but I can say it in Chihuahua, WOW WOW
or the bird outside my ears I think   YAW   YAW
on the dawn screened St. Dot's porch plunked on the cushion wrapped in
        the ersatz serape
huge iterating CAW inside my ear canal
or in the redwoods as humungous dark green leaves emitted like pearls
the sparrow is pecking the gravel
what is today's word? (What is checkwriter you ask)

an enigma into which howling trash and pearls pour, nope, today's word
is fatidic. huh?
light pours crenellated or floated by breath into the head in at the eyes and
        belly
a pool where thoughts float, tread water kick and scream their bellies bulge
        I shake
my white locks at the runaway sun
WOW WOW   YAW   YAW   not
a problem?
Of, relating to, or characterized by prophecy; prophetic.
so the caw sweeping through the green pearled air really was outside me, or
        the opposite:
fatidic as fatidic
does

CAW. my salutary poof. I sound my barbaric poof over the yawps of the
        world
detritus my breath screen   thinking splayed out like a Chinese scroll made
        of mud

and occasional light, thwacking like the beaver's paddle tail:
this is silly. back to the things themselves:
palm, palm, roof (white rubber-tec or what's it called), distant mountain:
O you to whom apostrophe is not
modern, and if I'm Keats
my face cracked open being the sparrow as light pours through melting it
          and pooling like Terminator Two into the bird's molded face no
          face its side-head eyes and underfluff pouring congealed into beak:
          peck. he said pecking about the gravel. what am I looking for
in there?
I do not seek I find. YAW. CAW. WOW WOW.

January 17, 2006

*

google latest American fatality Iraq:
oh shit   I forgot American.
the site is run by 16 researchers
largely academics
and musicians
also developed a JavaScript Web counter
can be added to any Web page to show the latest fatality estimates.

LET ME ENTER THE IRAQ BODY COUNT WEBSITE

Min 28,065 Max 31,653

U.S. Army officials said 22-year-old Pvt. Jonathan Pfender, of Evansville,
        Ind., was killed when an explosive device went off near his humvee

Pfender served with the 101st Airborne Division stationed in Fort
        Campbell.

His mother, Peggy Hammond, said her son will remain close to her in spirit.

"He's always with me," she said. "I can kiss him anytime I want, and he is
      close to my heart and he is never leaving my side."

*

It is I, Walt Whitman.

I'm Rilke now my face cracks flows and morphs, we're pecking companionably
      about the gravel what are we seeking, I do not seek I find, but Rilke,
      birdlike, gets busy & seeks:

year that rose longer you
vanish, blossom memory. poetry obeys
to trace each lightly
it looks, finds, stays.

days his word flows with other need
not will, he is Orpheus singing
for us. Can his overstepping our moment
erect names passed through a gravestone?

to few comes this lyre's
just rose. let in, we
understand, never to disappear.
his strings move here.

he hands you no
beyond, life wherever it is, and the no.

*

a song by Tenney now:
Yo ho. Sing Yorp. Wow wow.

*

FORTUNE
huh? how could you hear the curved bill thrasher through the wall
or the cactus wren again
O Rene Magritte I guess like mine the walls of your room are penetrable and
       full of clouds
which I correctly called "brick clouds" in my last book *Home on the Range*
       do you
understand why Rene? "Apostrophe's forbidden," you say
leaning like a brick through distance as clouds right into my room.
my face cracked. along the soft cold sand of the wash bottom, sluicing my
       bare feet,
myriad well anyway many branches and leaves greeted me with their gaze
       and let me go, I would never pass that way again
So I nodded to them as they would also never reappear
a god to a god somewhere
in Emerson you can read that remark, this isn't a pipe
It's wind. through the glass upper balcony window the palm's fronds hop
       and flutter a little in it
and the lower scrub hunkers, down beyond there's another wash
full of snakes in summer & also now in winter we presume (me and Rene)
could my face crack into that? packed-in dreaming reptile dreams wedged in
       cold sand among the various chilly rocks, all of which are soft
o rock blossoms
apostrophes are not permitted on the funicular   reptilian either
ensconced a frozen slither now in sand
theta-waving your warm weather death each grain

fallen from space (ghost snow falls through the void)

a pattern otherwise peculiar to those who turn out to be zen masters

quaint expression WHHHHH! O emergent reptilian apostrophe, snake
 song

by the road to the contagious hospital, maybe not, it might

be different spiky and fierce like everything else in Arizona, patches of
 standing

water? O you who are dear to my heart and can take the place of Rene
 Magritte:

brick (the rest is silence). Shut up now Maggie I'm writing. WOW WOW
 WOW.

& the chihuahua king answers in the same point type: WOW. WOW WOW.
 Each one according to his nature. I have tried to keep them from
 falling.

your face cracks. thank you Charles Kraitsir insane lord of all phonemes
 channeled by Henry David Thoreau: the sand warms and flows gl,
 gl, gla; glu (a cold snap): thick stunned muscle rattler shivering,
 emerging his head flecked with bright damp warming grains

fuck!

the Freudian enigma of when I'll actually see it (getting ready

to have been frightened) and the actual WHHHHHHH! from

under the analytic couch for instance--cry out, and run! I've actually been
 on two funiculars:

up Montserrat (warm reddish rock) and up Mont Blanc, a blank of like they
 say

blown snow and sheet ice, like the other guy's "decaying never to be
 decayed," but calm

and fiercer despite the vertigo I walked the low edgy parapets leaning over

for hours, Pat scuttled down, then back on solid ground I did the tipsy
 tinkerbell residual javelina shuffle vertiginous tiptoe like I could
 fall off the earth, walking

around Switzerland. I didn't. O eponymous snow snake of Mont Blanc

and red snake of Montserrat, I greet you

at the beginning of a great career, which nonetheless must have had

a long foreground somewhere (seen from the lower reaches of the
          funicular)
no three. right here the Mt. Lemmon ski lift, extremely scary w/ my vertigo
          and worse my daughter riding next to me without it on the little
          wandering airborne plank, "save what is with the breezes blown"
          leaning over the no edge like a book
dropped over the roof's edge itching you follow your hand which follows the
          book dive
over the edge to

grab it I saved Dennis once
out the fifteenth floor window of my house (hi Dennis)
he leaned back kidding around in the chair grabbed
at the sides of the window frame, laughing   not panicked
and missed   or horrible
David's sister really did fall through the loose window in Chicago
and die   the unhinged jaws of the Airshaft Snake
lifted & swallowed her whole
who am I
I thought it was about birds! Emptiness   and cloud bricks of the wall your
          face could morph into the beak and caw, not
WHHHH! unhinging swallowing space
"when all the stars are mute"
yet. well,
the Mission snake tried to eat the baby birds
as I have recorded
and had to back down
the tree (losing face   David said sheep have no tact)   O face:
but these are words! dissolving
funicular be still! Sway
                    like the mind
twinkled by wind and thought
in the clear snow and rocky air
cold sand

through which the snake stirs but not
yet.

January 19, 2006

          *

We interrupt this program
for a message from Bin Laden:

The soldier has no solution
except to commit suicide.
There is no difference between this criminality
and Saddam's criminality
they have used burning chemical acids and drills on their joints
they sometimes use the drills on their heads until they die
for their own private, suspect reasons
Bush announced the end of major operations
in that fake, ridiculous show aboard the aircraft carrier
with the tenfold number of dead and wounded who were killed in the smaller
          operations
The operations are under preparation and you will see them in your homes
          the minute they are through
results of polls please those who are sensible, Bush's opposition to them is
          a mistake
this shows the errors of Bush's statement -- the one that slipped from him
          -- which is at the heart of polls calling for withdrawing the troops
It is better that we (Americans) don't fight Muslims on their lands and that
          they don't fight us on ours
We don't mind offering you a long-term truce
on fair conditions that we adhere to. We are a nation
that God has forbidden
to lie and cheat. Finally,

I say that war will go either in our favor or yours. A swimmer in the ocean
does not fear the rain. Your minds will be troubled and your lives
        embittered
We were patient in fighting the Soviet Union with simple weapons for 10
        years
and we bled their economy
and now they are nothing.
You have tried to prevent us from leading a dignified life,
but you will not be able to prevent us from a dignified death.
In that there is a lesson for you.
As for us,
we have nothing to lose.

*

Senator Laura Bush? President Says Never

The Bush administration offered its fullest defense to date of the National
Security Agency's domestic eavesdropping program, saying that
authorization from Congress to deter terrorist attacks "places the president
at the zenith of his powers in authorizing the N.S.A. activities."

Mr. Bush sang his wife's praises on Thursday, noting

that she had just returned from Africa,
that she was involved in advocating literacy programs and that

he had delegated to her the first decision he had to make after winning the
        presidency

the design of the rug in the Oval Office.

FORTUNE?

No frays at your edges now
it's scary. What did Rilke have in mind?

Silence is the shadow. Throat presses
sepulcher, voice becomes
that sensuous praising, god's deathless passing,
fruit to any mouth.

In his mortal decay, stone's fallen vineyard,
die all hills ripened whenever wine was ripe,
the dead with that ore
of glorious heart. all of us

summoned from the gods
came from the south like kings
into his grip
far from the doors of inexhaustible praise.

* is this the beginning or is something missing?
Nietzsche said I must be the subject of my propositions   laugh laugh
there's no remainder. John said it's a collection of grievances and
          accomplishments, but mostly
grievances. In Tucson the Dalai Lama said
anger focuses the field to the point of a single cause sometimes
useful often not. What do you say? I say stay
stay, stay, stay, streak intrinsicality no
that was David. what do I say?

John from Falcon Pools is re-opening the broken ball valve and then

                leaving it open
and I will learn to by-pass closing it

What is that under your robe?

Norman said the last one is delightful and restless not about words though
                run through them
which was very kind
one skewer
better than one finger
anyway easier on the hand
like one hand

the clouds which are lowering a little now with patches of gray livid is too
                strong a word were so floaty earlier this morning, soft
and buoyant as if in the air is water koan but no
the breeze was soft and wet but not like water, like spring she said, house
                rules are to remove the name
della primavera trasportata al
morale, ta-ra! ta-ra!

the hills to the southwest hover in softness still, gouached out more the
                further your eye goes, limit emptied into the color and texture of
                low sky
I think it's poplars thrust up thin and wispy in the mediate foreground
or cypresses or cedars
it comes out of me as tree blather
the hills shed bulk (David Antin said all the mountains look like tablecloths
                in late Cezanne) and all the rocks are soft, fallen from space like
                basinets
the green blue yellow kid-slide is held by the koan mu, no to you
americano camerado loveable huggable emily brown
the dog barks to say John is done in dog, I think
miss brown to you

these tessellated distractions are what I say I think

there's the bell

nope he can't fix it

it's open but can't be by-passed during cleaning without flooding the filter

so the big question is whether the American Home Shield warranty will
        cover the repair even though part of the pipe is underground and
        needs digging up and the spa will have to be drained to allow it

Americans are fat lazy stupid and pampered

thought Nietzsche as a general rule & fret endlessly about nothing   laugh
        laugh

no remainder   over their pump propositions and their filter ones, and the
        proposition concerning what they think he thinks and the one
        which posits him laughing

a general regress as the mirror falls into the mirror

GA!

a god nods to a god

nothing tips hat to nothing

Lee Konitz laughed because I sang "I kick my ass as I pass" I was trying to
        do Billie Holiday

she actually sang "I tip my hat as I pass"

WOW WOW

don't you all get too familiar

some day

what do you say? all this junk?

What is that under your robe

I dunno sir.

is there a manuscript? I dunno but if there is

it bleeds into the clouds and low hills to which it intends to refer

oh bullshit   the clouds are transfixed momentarily by sun and illumined
        the light pours around them at the frayed edge no and through
        them a little bit too

I am nothing but the subject of my propositions

glug glug glug

today that's what I say: glug. What is that

under your robe? glug.
but

not tomorrow:
it will cut to the marrow.
what?

intimate
she said.

January 25, 2006

*

You just don't get to prefer, OK? OK today I seem to want to stoke the
        proposition maker
baffled? balked? bent to the very earth?
Or I want some propositions to stoke the other maker thing
Which isn't another thing
it's me, no, what is it you want
These are propositions
the downstairs imac was making them ad nauseum this morning too
        sorry I mean ad infinitum eerie walking through the tv nook to
        make more latte & hear it declaiming to itself in the empty room
I must have been empty is poetry

catechism interiorized? or to you?
adrenal tumor . . .
Mr. Abbas also had words of calm for Israel on Wednesday
And so we can imagine that physics varies from one universe to another.
Can his overstepping our moment
The Kurds are a non-Arabic people who speak
a language related to Persian.
erect names passed through a gravestone?
wolves excavate dens to give birth and raise a litter in. A Wolf Dunn is a

place where ideas are born and grow.

"If I am inclined to suppose that a mouse has come into being by
spontaneous generation out of grey rags and dust, I shall do well
to examine those rags very closely to see how a mouse may have
hidden in them, how it may have got there and so on. But if I am
convinced that a mouse cannot come into being from these things,
then this investigation will perhaps be superfluous."

The Surrealist has judged the mind. he does not recognize any thought as
his own. His thought does not fashion for him a world to which he
reasonably assents.

The Palestinian Central Elections Commission said that Hamas won
76 seats and Fatah 43 in the 132-seat Palestinian Legislative
Council.

But first we must learn to understand what it is that opposes such an
examination of details in philosophy.

put oneself in the right frame of mind. No Surrealist believes in the
effectiveness of the mind as spur, the mind as guillotine, the mind
as judge, the mind as doctor,

It is notorious for its generous payments to the families of suicide bombers
on one hand while in an attempt to change its image in the eyes
of the west Hamas is also paying a media consultant £100,000
to persuade Europeans and Americans that it is not a group of
religious fanatics who relish suicide bombings and hate Jews

After Palestine, the Zionists aspire to expand from the Nile to the
Euphrates. When they will have digested the region they
overtook, they will aspire to further expansion, and so on. Their
plan is embodied in the "Protocols of the Elders of Zion", and
their present conduct is the best proof of what we are saying

The various schools of thought are not always in direct competition with
one another -- even though they sometimes reach differing
conclusions.

An important failing of the ice-skater analogy is that the exchange of
bowling balls is always repulsive

One of the most difficult or misleading aspects of Wittgenstein's

Philosophical Investigations is the way in which he uses multiple
voices to converse with himself. To have a sense of understanding
Wittgenstein, you need to be able to hear these different voices.
I believe in your love.
I believe
biscuit tortoni   35c per portion
On a second trip, as a teen-ager, bin Laden joined some friends and
relatives on a big-game safari in East Africa.
And let's give Barry Bonds a few more years to put the fear of God into the
pitchers.
".....there is a great variety of criteria for personal 'identity'.
Now which of them determines my saying that 'I' am in pain? None."

The world
is all
that is
the case.

No.

January 26, 2006

*

1.25

Then your altered flesh like a flower
burst out, listening
hesitant bronze by shadows darkly
filled, so early your

blood flowed, gleamed. Pulses
pausing, unearthly
youth taken away
show it to darkness

fell altered from the high young flesh
dear flesh possessed again
whose body
interrupted by downfall,

companion already cast by shadows darkly possessed,
filled inconsolably near terrible dominions, open, pounding,
unsubduable grieving door

*

A federal judge blasted former EPA chief Christine Todd Whitman on
        Thursday for reassuring New Yorkers soon after the Sept. 11,
        2001, terror attacks that it was safe to return to their homes and
        offices while toxic dust was polluting the neighborhood.
"No reasonable person would have thought that telling thousands of
        people that it was safe to return to lower Manhattan, while
        knowing that such return could pose long-term health risks and
        other dire consequences, was conduct sanctioned by our laws,"
        the judge said.
saying the Environmental Protection Agency chief knew that the collapse
        of the twin towers released tons of hazardous materials into the
        air.
Whitman had no comment, a spokeswoman said. A Justice Department
        spokesman said the government had no comment.
Batts noted that the EPA and Whitman said repeatedly — beginning just
        two days after the attacks — that the air appeared safe to breathe.
        The EPA's internal watchdog later found that the agency, at the
        urging of White House officials, gave misleading assurances.
a public official cannot be held personally liable for putting the public in
        harm's way unless the conduct was so egregious as "to shock
        the contemporary conscience." Given her role in protecting the
        health and environment for Americans, Whitman's reassurances
        after Sept. 11 were "without question conscience-shocking,"

Batts said.
But I shall be good health to you nevertheless,
And filter and fibre your blood.
If you want me again look for me under your bootsoles.

*

(1.8)

Deities may be still as she is. Night
dawns in our heart
upon the glittering stream
lifts a constellation

awkward stone
night after night
only sky.
voice

wept. Longing still learns
praising the hidden stream
the bright heart
upon the altar--

watching over
the fountain   counts the ancient beads.

June 12, 2006

Fundamentalists picket military rites

COLUMBUS, Ohio – States are rushing to limit when and where people may protest at funerals – all because of a small fundamentalist Kansas church whose members picket soldiers' burials, arguing that Americans are dying for a country that harbors homosexuals.

During the 1990s, the Westboro Baptist Church of Topeka, Kan., went around picketing the funerals of AIDS victims with protest signs that read, "God Hates Fags." But politicians began paying more attention recently when church members started showing up at the burials of soldiers and Marines killed in Afghanistan and Iraq.

he is trying to achieve a balance that respects "the rights of families to bury their dead in peace."

The church has about 75 members. The church is an independent congregation that preaches a literal reading of the Bible.

states cannot interfere with their message that the soldiers were struck down by God because they were fighting for a country that harbors homosexuals and adulterers.

Jean went to his funeral an hour early to avoid protesters. They were already across the road, holding signs that read "God Hates Fags" and "God Made IEDs," a reference to roadside bombs.

Legislation against funeral protests was also introduced in West Virginia after a small knot of protesters from Westboro Baptist demonstrated outside a memorial for the 12 men killed in the Sago Mine disaster. The protesters held signs reading, "Thank God for Dead Miners," "God Hates Your Tears" and "Miners in Hell," arguing that the miners' deaths were a sign of God's wrath at America for tolerating gays.

*

PROFLIGATE?   FORTUNE?
I won't make any graven images today
apostrophe you're dangerous
when I practice the koan NO I will not have a single thought fall slanting

across the mind
if I do I'll fuck myself in the ass for penance
we're all crazy
my son fell down and dropped the leash my red heeler ran straight up to a
      tiny strange dog, flipped and bit him
hard causing $464 worth of puncture wounds (see spreadsheet)
what proposition was she entertaining?
the desert white cottontail hops through the underbrush pale matte because
      of the clouds next to the tossed beercan
easing the mind   as Williams might say
I will make no graven image of the prophet
I will just burn European embassies to the ground
a little random juice here
after all   not random just holes
underworld of the basin by hole under results
dharma crafts the revered American practice breaking your critical stick the
      cards succumb
underworld the lightbulb to sense rooms, under intelligent people they off
      his face into the dots
crafts graceful accessories Thailand great frame the doctor ordered
voila the perpetual graven image factory, and the graven image of bowing
      to it
& up under it the rabbit scurrying across part of it over there through the
      gray blur you can see the cloudlight again the spellchecker hates
      that graven image the air is warm and wet
a panorama   scroll
of mind flapping light and late morning dew
before writing down graven images
after sitting in them Mohammed
I great you at the beginning of a great career lookout a-
postrophe Monk
said epistrophy
what's that? profligate as
profligate do?

((Rhet.) A figure in which successive clauses end with the same word or affirmation; e. g., «Are they Hebrews? so am I. Are they Israelites? so am I.» 2 Cor. xi. 22.))

February 9, 2006

*

What are you doing over there in the corner again?
I'm building a nation in Iraq. I call it nation building.
What is that dead fork in your hand?
Nothing again nothing. I said I'm nation-building dammit.
Are you a roadside bombing terrorist?
No I am the President I'm leading one nation and building another.
Where are you leading it?
I'm leading it to the other one to build it.
And where are you leading the one you're building?
I'm leading it to the other one that's this one to lead it, and I will make it
        drink.
Are you leading it to water?
Oil.
Do they mix?
When the terrorists mix it, it explodes!
And you?
Even as it is said, as in the beginning so in the end, world unto world: what
        does it profit a man to mix oil in his gas tank if his axle is evil?
Who said that?
Sadman, The Aye, I Told You of North Korea.
What's your favorite book?
Windows on the World for Dummies.
Is it a dirty book?
What am I doing over there in the corner again?
Why don't you go ask Dick?

You little slut! Aren't you glad that in America we can debate these issues
        freely?
Yes.
Me too. Want to join me in the corner now?
What are you doing?
Come in under the shadow of this red rock, and I will show you something.
They called me the hyacinth girl.
And I knew nothing, looking into the heart of light, the silence.
Where's that?
Iraq, you dummy.
Hosannah! You're the rapper, Ice George.
Get jiggy wid' it.
Exeunt Omnes, singing: Dada said there'll be days like this. Saddam said
        there'll be days like this. 'Sama said there'll be days like this. But I
        doan worry, cause.
Big enough to include the name of every drink served in every tavern in
        America?
You bet.

February 13, 2006

*

Today muddy center of being bumps the oleander's air the leaves thump and
        the air jostles lightly, being is a ball
the cyst needs to be removed
the leaves get fluttered up, rough trade
a pleasure for the oleander too it's plain to see
(Maple, I see you have
a squirrel in your crotch—

blushing and penetrated, splayed
air the mind's mud scroll flapping
And you have a woodpecker

in your hole, Sycamore)
eureka, it's valentine's day, chocolate, flowers
and wind   bussing my body all over with soft balsamic busses thanks Walt
        be laureate of oleanders now
the flippin / funicular again
Snakes are venomous too
not their blossoms but their bite
no the leaves make your mouth froth fanged head
stirs in stony sleep in the wash under sand, seismic
shift to nearby mites and midges
the warm air is heaven
Philip Whalen orotund Buddha snapped by Ginsberg American boy
in kimono writing in zen notebook or scanning his ledgers, sweet fat roshi
        accountant
tutelary deity but the genius loci
isn't fat but fanged
actually not so warm before dawn it was balmy in the ready to be lifted dark,
        frayed at the edges pale gray rising
minutiae I can't spell it of the actual as glory, I'd like to get laid
the newly ensconsed canvas chair on the balcony feels like an egg
roc egg I never sat in
the palo verdes also take it in stride
the snake climbed up the mesquite after eggs at the Mission but backed
        down or off
I wrote that
a couple years ago oops the cell phone is buzzing in my pocket like a fly
don't answer
more writing
before I was thinking about who I was when I wrote about the Mission I
        think
now I'll think about who we were years before when the snake did that there
        and we watched
from the shine hill, what an awkward phrase, maybe in wind, it was dusk the
        phone again! soft leagues of air over the valley

46

dry damp ocean desert breeze, cool heatwaves scud, what could the snake
       see
eggs, wind, probably the air too along its scales where the mesquite bark
       was rough like a bad shave or a good backscratcher, a rope burn
       a scrape from sliding home "that last is surely wrong" Kenneth
       wrote somewhere
now he's dead
the fly's in my pocket wrestling something hard now who was it saw
the fly's eyes blink a hundred times a second in neo-realist detail outside the
       breathing tent I was in a fly zone
Iraq was in a no-fly zone
now it's exploding
daily who were they
when Saddam lay them down on a pillow of poison gas
when we piled them up to pretend to be fucked at Abu Ghraib
when Al Quaida's scrubs blew them up in mosques by the sides of roads
       while the wind hopped up whatever kinds of leaves are there the air
       was being's mud
and the sky changed
moment by moment there and over here
I'm your valentine today
in muddy air the sun spanks
awake through the filter of air-swathed clouds you know
today the snake says yes
is a good story.

February 14, 2006

*

Hey Democritus
whiz aaiiiiieeeeeeee!
I'm made of fraying chainmail
if so I'll collapse at the bottom in a glittering heap

with a little viscous rebound resettling like in the crash dummy
     commercials
but shinier
wwwhhhhooooooooooo!
I need earmuffs
clinamen dammit why don't you look where you're going
some plunging atoms are boinging like soft bees in a rubberized clog dance
     right next to me
coalescing into Harold Bloom
thanks to the spellchecker
his tie goes shooting upward past his neck like a noose in a cosmic draft
O romantic cosmic funicular
keep falling shit look out BANG the chainmail goes gooey in the friction of
     plunged
stuff I'm silver metal bubblegum now glommed onto Harold's face
so I'm John's octopus, I mean Harold's John's octopus
Iraq comes ricocheting toward us from the right (quick IED disposal
     calculus)
a roadside bomb explodes in the void below your feet rushing off to the left-
     hand void now
I vow to save all beings
yours truly the chainmail gum
waking to slithering & fangs luminous
noumena I'll miss you apostrophe

hurtles up too in the windy rage ur-cosmos
I greet you at the end of a great career
which nonetheless must have had a long foreground somewhere
the floating delicate light on bushes and grasses
kinetic testicles scrotal sac wind thanks Walt   .
you walk through the wash sand on the wind hill outside Santa Fe the
     creosote bush looks at you a final time
& the sand does, and the firs
in the gently falling koan about snow

"which is not falling in that other place," hence falling
in that other place, this is how it is for me signed
the bubblegum
something wicked this way comes
shrieking up through wind but can this be, if there's no air
but there's snow here
& in the cross-drift rising & falling it floats & hovers buoyed by the air that
       isn't here like real snow hopping lightly horizontal for awhile
it is real snow
lighting up the void the moonlight catches it from the top and side and the
       underside
tender void
through which the soft rocks fall
approaching light
speed bump   I greet you um I'm turning into Walt again great rock me in
       billowy drowse I can repay you
coin of the realm which is breath, exhaling thoughts to the vanished air they
       hover and pulse as snow
Richard Hell and the Voidoids?
nope Willie Nelson singing Moonlight in Vermont again
icy finger waves? I see finger waves? I don't get it
a snowdrift ripples through my face, cold wavy muscles they pass it along
       into chattered air
morphed mats of light
telephone I don't think Democritus can be the origin of democracy?
there goes the other sun in a ball
turned into snow
and mossy scabs of the worm fence, and heaped stones, and elder and
       mullein and pokeweed
the chainmail came from the stars I mean it was them
I came from mud
falling in wind now glittering
like the mind
that made all this

at 11:41 a.m.
in sun
through the ambient cloud-filter again

February 15, 2006

*

Hey Dick

get tired
of shooting
yourself in the
foot yet?

2/17/06

*

BAGHDAD, Iraq, Feb. 15 [2006] – Late Saturday night, on the eve of a crucial vote to choose Iraq's next prime minister, a senior Iraqi politician's cellphone rang. A supporter of the Shiite cleric Moktada al-Sadr was on the line with a threat.

"He said that there's going to be a civil war among the Shia" if Mr. Sadr's preferred candidate was not confirmed, the politician said.

Less than 12 hours later, Mr. Sadr got his wish. The widely favored candidate lost by one vote, and Ibrahim al-Jaafari, the interim prime minister, was anointed as Iraq's next leader.

"Everyone was stunned; it was a coup d'état," said the politician.

It was a crowning moment for Mr. Sadr, whose sudden rise to political power poses a stark new set of challenges for Iraq's fledgling democracy. The man who led the Mahdi Army militia's two deadly uprisings against American troops in 2004 now controls 32 seats in Iraq's Parliament, enough to be a kingmaker. He has an Islamist vision of Iraq's future, and is implacably hostile to the Iraqis closest to the United States.

*

our new home it's exciting and new
so come along we're expecting you

*

OUR AMERICA

I was teaching Amerikanistik at University of Stuttgart in spring 1991, (first) Iraq invasion ("desert storm"; by 1992 the Arizona football team's defense was "desert swarm" in the press guide), hot on the hot (or cool) heels of reunification. Mostly poetry but also a little film (*Easy Rider*, *Deerhunter*, *Apocalypse Now*) plus American English. I brought articles from American papers, Pat Benetar on a walkman (yes I believe there comes a time when everything just falls in line) and one day the class tumbled giddily onto American racism (Arizona's Damon Stoudamire athletic scholarships graduation rates hypocrisy exploitation) . Whole lotta shakin' goin' on: many puffed up preening young Germans (no surprise) but (surprise) "we're not like that here," and then "that could never happen here." And it was the invasion, they were right (while being wrong): a sunny, cheerful room of smug twenty-year old new Europeans, you could hear the virtual Euros already clinking in their pockets fingered in anticipatory enjoyment of a perfectly morally sanitized liberal consumerism ("not like American materialism"). One Marxist demurred (trashed guest-arbeiter Turks her evidence). On the trains coming home from touristing weekends, drunken footballers singing Deutschland Uber Alles and kicking some occasional insufficiently Deuschlander ass, leg-sprawling skinheads pumping beer sunbathed their retro Nazi tattooed torsos (so history is nothing but fashion Fred?) on the big lake boats, windblown and cloudblown. On the way to the train in Tubingen "Nazis Raus." East German and East European academics came to the annual Amerikanistic conference in Muenster (say cheese) for the first time, & were uber Germanic (40 minutes reviewing the scholarship, two minutes rushed & tremulously proffered individual interpretation). In the train stations everyone younger than me looked self-assuredly hipper than anyone in America, BMWs and Mercedes were driven by all, boutiques full of chic shirts with California labels unavailable in the States, fettuccini with goranzola creamsauce in every bowl, where no one's taxes footed the military bill. Everyone older shambled around struggling to look inconspicuous in their leg irons, their old people ties, hats, formal sport coats, too-heavy dress coats in the new spring air. A few years before they'd been stooped over groping for the wadded up world of their lost youth, thrown into the dark corner now with the Deutschmarks (not yet, but soon!), lifers doing minimum security time while the other wall came tumbling down. All along the watchtower, princes kept the view. Two riders were approaching. The wind began to howl. But you and I we've been through this. Hey Be-attle: It's 2006 and we're, ack ack ack ack, back in the, ack ack ack ack, back in the, back in the—we're back in Iraq.

February 18, 2006

*

Fredric Jameson I greet you
(need totality?   periploi)

Did anyone
find Fenton's red jacket? dinner
for the finder!
thanks Fenton.

red jacket I greet you
following a long foreground draped on Fenton
gone to red jacket bardo
a kind of karmic
laundromat a comforter flung over Sal Mineo's wandering ghost   I am a
            sock I have come to tell you all
Plato's parable (banana fana fo fock, fee
fie mo mock, clock
map? boomerang walkabout periplum apostrophe epistrophe Monk
said there's always music just most
don't hear it hear it

February 18, 2006

*

Police found at least 40 bodies – shot and discarded – in Baghdad
Apart from his swipe at Iran, Bush painted a picture of progress in Iraq,
Bush said that some of the most powerful "improvised explosive devices"
            (known as IEDs) in Iraq contained "components that came from
            Iran."

President Bush today refused to rule out a U.S. nuclear strike to prevent
            Iran from developing atomic weapons, saying that "all options are
            on the table."

The United States wants to settle the Iran nuclear crisis through diplomacy
President George W. Bush said describing reports of plans to attack Iran as
            "wild speculation."
"The doctrine of prevention is to work together to prevent the Iranians from

having a nuclear weapon," Bush said

the use of tactical nuclear weapons is one option being considered by the
administration

"Nobody in the Pentagon," Hersh continued, "seriously thinks (the use
of tactical nuclear weapons) could be – it's an impossible option.
They (Pentagon planners) wanted to get rid of it (but) ... the White
House said, 'No.'

"Do the removal of Israel before it is too late and save yourself from the
fury of regional nations," the ultra-conservative president said. He
once again called the Holocaust a "fairy tale" and said Europeans
have become hostages of "Zionists" in Israel.

He also accused Europeans for not allowing "neutral scholars" to investigate
in Europe and make a scientific report on "the truth about the fairy
tale of Holocaust."

"How comes that insulting the prophet of Muslims worldwide is justified
within the framework of press freedom, but investigating about the
fairy tale Holocaust is not?" Ahmadinejad said.

Bush seems sincerely to see the world as a battleground between Good
and Evil, St Michael's angels against the forces of Lucifer. We're
gonna smoke out the Amalekites, send a posse after the Midianites,
smite them all and let God deal with their souls. Minds doped up on
this kind of cod theology have a hard time distinguishing between
Saddam Hussein and Osama bin Laden.

Some of Bush's faithful supporters even welcome war as the necessary
prelude to the final showdown between Good and Evil: Armageddon
followed by the Rapture.

In 2003, the Persian Gulf countries (Bahrain, Iran, Iraq, Kuwait, Qatar,

Saudi Arabia, and the United Arab Emirates) produced about 27% of the world's oil, while holding 57% (715 billion barrels) of the world's crude oil reserves.

BigChurch.com bringing people together in love and faith
"I met Shawn on BigChurch.com and knew Jesus was in our relationship. Shawn is such an amazing blessing in my life. Thanks BigChurch!!"

- Slik101

Map of the Iran Iraq war
Insurgents posing as police destroyed the golden dome of one of Iraq's holiest Shiite shrines Wednesday, setting off an unprecedented spasm of sectarian violence.

For George W Bush it may have been the mother of all political backdrops. The US President made a dramatic entry onto an aircraft carrier to declare victory in Iraq. He stopped short of declaring the Iraq war officially over and also vowed America's war on terror that began on September 11, 2001 will continue. The speech marks the beginning of a new phase for the US in Iraq. It also sends an important message to the American public that the President's attention is shifting back from the war to the troubled economy.

Offering a robust reaffirmation of the Bush administration's doctrine of pre-emptive action to deal with threats to national security, the latest four-yearly National Security Strategy published by the White House declares

Nobel Peace Prize nominee Dr Helen Caldicott fears US President George Bush's re-election will lead to Armageddon

The French president, Jacques Chirac, has threatened states which support terrorist attacks on France and its strategic interests, or which contemplate the use of weapons of mass destruction, with retaliatory nuclear strikes. He announced this new definition of French defence strategy on Thursday at the nuclear powered submarine base,

"We will continue to hunt down the enemy before he can strike," he told the cheering officers and sailors aboard the ship.

Earlier, Mr Bush's spokesman Ari Fleischer

Earlier, Mr Bush's spokesman Scott McLellan

In naming Snow, president chooses a press secretary unafraid to

"They want people to express their opinions," Snow said of the famously insular Bush White House. "You're not coming here to drink the Kool-Aid, you're coming to serve the president."

Did sales worldwide of Kool Aid go up or down after the mass suicide in Jamestown, Guyana with Kool Aid?

Greetings Jaana,

While Kool-Aid was not used in the Jonestown massacre, as many say, this news did play havoc on the sales of Kool-Aid. I have just this one source that is anecdotal in nature, but I would assume it is true:

Insound.com - "The Causey Way" (mentions Kool Aid briefly, saying that sales went down in 1978-80)

The 80's ad campaign with the Kool Aid Man mascot was Kool-Aid's attempt to get itself back in good condition. It worked, as I assume, having drank much Kool-Aid myself in the 80's (and I'm still alive, LOL).

Earlier, Mr Bush's spokesman Ari Fleischer warned that the president's speech would not mark the end of hostilities "from a legal point of view".

In TV and print ads, Kool-Aid Man was known for bursting suddenly through walls, seemingly summoned by the making and imbibing of Kool-Aid by kids. His **catch-phrase** is "Oh, yeah!"

A **catch phrase** is a phrase or expression that is spontaneously popularized after a critical amount of widespread repeated usage in everyday conversation (i.e., it "catches" on). Also called a *memetic phrase*, catch phrases often originate in **popular culture**

Popular culture, or **pop culture**, is the **vernacular** (people's) **culture** that prevails in any given **society**.

The term "**Manifest Destiny**", for example, was a catch phrase of the mid-nineteenth century, coined by journalist **John O'Sullivan** in an **editorial** in **1845**. The phrase spread so quickly that people soon forgot who first introduced the term. In time, "Manifest Destiny" ceased to be a catch phrase, instead becoming a standard historical term, and a permanent part of the **lexicon** of U.S. history.

Some catch phrases become the "trademark" or defining characteristic of the person or character with whom they originated.

I want justice. And there's an old poster out west, that I recall, that said, ``Wanted, Dead or Alive."

Just remember, all I'm doing is remembering when I was kid. I remember that I used to put out there in the old West a "wanted" posted. It said, "Wanted, Dead or Alive." All I want and America wants is to see them brought to justice. That's what we want.

In the **professional wrestling** arena, catch phrases are often essential to a wrestler's **gimmick**. Some, such as **The Rock**'s "Can you smell what The Rock is cookin'" and **"Stone Cold" Steve Austin**'s "Austin 3:16" and "That's the bottom line, 'cause Stone Cold said so" achieved exceptional popularity. These phrases have proceeded to symbolize pro wrestling itself, even after the active careers of their associated star figures have ended.

In terms of Mr. bin Laden himself, we'll get him running. We'll smoke him
        out of his cave, and we'll get him eventually.
It's barbaric behavior. They slit throats of women on airplanes in order to
        achieve an objective that is beyond comprehension. And they like
        to hit, and then they like to hide out.
But we're going to smoke them out.

Modern professional wrestling is a **performing art**, where the participants
        create an entertainment show simulating a **combat sporting**
        match. The level of realism can vary

April 27, 2006

*

Yippee. Let's plunge all the little fuckers into friggin' Civil War!
Let's frag their tiny Shiite and Sunni asses!
Today's experiment: what will the poem be like if written while eating
        Chinese take-out?
more attractive postmodern disjunctive patina etiology fiddled out of chop-
        sticks between bursts?
nouvelle bunker mentality (vide infra)
"ego scriptor"   a muddled Confucian
Taoist w/o portfolio
all the proscriptions fell open like fallen fruit
"the great periplum brings in the stars to our shore"

say to la cara, amo

"we're alive and we're dead
we think we're alive now and we'll be dead later but that's baloney"

back in the day they brought Coors to the President by private jet direct from Colorado

made great plans and penetrated inaudibly across the border   now it's a
       death museum (skulls and photos)

can it go on like this

some chicken lo mein some zen some reductio redacted

over on the zen list William just raised the topic of himself and the war

(just learned several months later his son is in Iraq)

my way is to bifurcate

some outrage from the internet, some looks over the foliate wash from the
       upstairs window after sitting

potentially pretty dangerous

blah blah blah

the enormous risk Jackson Pollock took using his drip technique

what a pity to say so

said the economical elder monk to the enthused newly enlightened younger
       monk who said

"everything is so beautiful"

and it is

ten years after the breeze-blown tent kept sliding a blurring membrane near
       my face

and the bird's wings made viscous tracks through slow air

I don't like the pineapple chunks (sneaked in) I like the peppers

elder monk POW (wow wow)

but the kicker is that story is held in words

koan rhyming poem

today that's what I say   so my little dog knows me

this is the end times? *Satyricon* aftermath along west 8th prosthetic rubber
       masks encasing every face

dark carnival street leer

but this one doesn't know he's encased in rubber

and wants to hear just so much

as sustains his let's say religious vision so his briefs

purvey briefly in his world

of necessity all goes well quod erat demonstrandum

"enjoying" the president's ear
like a bathroom wall
if then he hear
this sums the apparatus
comprised in prayer
it makes me think of porches
here's a true story:
the one thing that kept me from achieving a score high enough to join the
        foreign service was an inability to paraphrase clearly a speech by Al
        Haig in under 300 words
you don't get it?
apparently I didn't
a mind like a steel trap snagging a bush
no better than my President?
over on the zen list I got ripping along on *Civilization and Its Discontents*
        and the Dalai Lama
it makes sense if you think about it
the super-ego's severity inextricable from the tendency to war, it's not as
        silly as it sounds
the calibrated bobbin of self ratcheted to a very tight pinch, Yeatsian bobbin
        suddenly unwound
bashing whatever it clicks by
what the Dalai Lama did was cry
they asked "but what about self-hatred"
in his country people don't have it
he said   I don't believe that, but I kind of believe it
I'm a fucking idiot
anyway he doesn't have one
off to tell more lies John said he said or was that some other lama
Get with the program! But mommy that was a asshole. I think
I'll napalm and nuke their fucking Muslim asses? their Born Again asses?
        I'll napalm and nuke my father's son's sorry ass?
or else no one is here to be liking the pineapple yum

the pieces sproinging loose in dokusan popping my bedraggled mattress
    head (the spellchecker sneaked in springing but I caught its
    miserable spellchecking ass). it's interview now. When I couldn't
    answer that other koan
I yelled FUCK IT! inside my head for two full sits. Then that went away.
I threw the dishtowel at Sharon (in Cambridge) Claus Oldenburg must be
    alive and well somewhere and missed by twenty feet
the smallest sprout
shows there is really no death
Last week I banged the cereal box down in tiny rage on the self-checkout
    counter the fucking screen kept telling me PLACE ITEM ON
    SCALE duh   done, but not duly enough apparently
I read today about the massively destructive rage afflicting fully 5% of
    Americans (I did not receive
a summons). Dear William all that said I have not yet invaded Iraq
perhaps it's not so much rage then as a neo acceptable sociopathic disregard,
    cut with a dog-shreds-the-towel tenacity regarding one's views?
that's what I think.
I believe in your love (biscuit tortoni 35c per portion)
I am not opposed to light consensual s/m.
I am not opposed to removing the Burqua. (Burke? Bursa? Burma?)
I am not opposed to the internet, the Odyssey, the grasses, scrotal sac, wind,
    thanks Walt
U.S. OUT OF IRAQ.
because I peck about the gravel.
I don't like Wolfson or Weinberger
is you just don't get to prefer
Sigmund Freud, I greet you at the beginning of a great career.
Maitraya Buddha still to be born.

June 7, 2006

*

inter-
regnum

well
jejune in June:

"the rage of politics, the compassion of practice."
the politics of rage the practice of compassion   the practice of politics the
          rage of compassion   the politics of practice the compassion of
          rage
let it go. the sentences   adagios of islands
And onward   bells   poinsettia meadows
terror   snowy tides
the vortex of our graves
of lovers' hands
O seasons clear, and awe

Bind us in time

June 7, 2006

*

nick of time
five minute Buddha (w/o portfolio)
bind us in time
quick? but this is the green tree window (not the other window)
looking up through straggled star foliage crossed by strict simple principles
          (not out and down big vista to the wash & beyond the city A
          Mountain & beyond that Baboquivari)
box view flecked by hopping points of light   what's with the breezes blown
          (etcetera)
be tender. all debts public and private
come due, may come soon. so I'm with Norman,
see how far simple kindness carries you.

Several five hundred pound bombs just blew the bejeezus out of Abu Musab
    al-Zarqawi (made in America)
provoking if I may quote Martha Reeves dancing in the streets and apparently
    widespread Iraqi bubilation what a typo. hey nah, my boyfriend's
    back now you're gonna get a beatin' Hail to the Chief of dubious
    import
I missed the interview with Daniel Berg's father he didn't wish for his death

who beast their fucking plowshares into swords?
I did, said the little red hen.
I did, said the little punk bush.
I pray for the enlightenment of

ten minute Buddha. fortunes
all gone (there's a drawer somewhere crammed with fortunes but I can't find
    it)
O drawer Bardo
and the star leaves aren't hopping so much
O Iraqi palms and attendant lesser foliage
nope. star jasmine (nope)   Arabian jasmine (nope)   jasmine still to be
    born (nope)
last night's meditative hopped up excitement brimming with slowness inside
    it
burbles up again intense and lazy, subsides skitters or slips soothes plops
into what? calm again darkening among water lights
who let this into the house
someone with no form or shadow draws up the water from the well
two bell-cup flowers on the tree open and dangle down, more or less cheek
    by jowel
then nothing. comparatively speaking. jowl. several yellow flower surfaces
    slide or hop up or down (slow boinging branch), catching the glint
    then slipping free, softened to dull butter petal texture
how kind of the state of Arizona, I mean the State, the funding arm
dying a slow inevitable post-fordist death but still full of unlikely barely

intended grace-notes.
an entire photograph of rubble, deathsite. They say
Zarqawi was a thug, a rapist, "loser."
They say he was a winner
who forever
changed the face of terror
upstaging Bin Laden
with sharper internet acumen.
now summer is i'cumin in
lude sing cuckoo. I saw
an extremely boisterous double yellow-head amazon this morning at OK
      Feed
trilling, hello-ing, fluffing, then hanging his head upside down like a butter
      flower
but not much like it. with quizzical inverted head he kept his amazon eye
      on me
not cautiously, but what? parrotly. I peck about the gravel
ego scriptor, with my head flipped up I fix you with the poet's inverted eye.
The military macaw
in native habitat
takes care of all his food needs in a nano, plays more
than most other species combined. Newlywed jihadists (NPR)
watch Zarqawi beheading Berg
on their wedding night, in English we would say
the piece of resistance. that's genius.
And the Eagle clutches its arrows fiercely, earth's most terrible cliché,
O world fear the might and guile and utter ineptitude of the United States
      of America
in its long-term tenacity but especially its present besotted idiocy.
welcome back ye colde war binaries, oh Johnnie (without 'em) we hardly
      knew ya. icy polar logic
leaves me cold. the poem shudders for other reasons too
jalopy shaking out some other encrusted selfoid.
the flowers hop and brush the long green pointy leaves, then settle down.

everything perfect as it is? ok.
or as you put it (that's not me),
"still no difficulty has entered." that's the missing fortune
settling toward tenderness, ferocious and soft.
or also (verbatim) "don't look a gifted horse in the mouth."

June 9, 2006

*

We Welcome You
to Today's Episode of
NACHTRAGLIKEIT

Speaking from the Rose Garden , President Bush praised the U.S.-led
coalition for continuing to pursue Zarqawi through "years of near-misses
and false leads."
"Through his every action, he sought to defeat America and our coalition
partners and turn Iraq into a safe haven from which al-Qaeda could wage its
war," Bush said. ". . . Now Zarqawi has met his end, and this violent man will
never murder again."

June 9, 2006

*

anticipatory birthday poem
fortune or t-shirt?
age and treachery will always overcome youth and skill   fifty and shifty

now sixty what?
what are we to understand concerning mortalia?
I greet you at the beginning of a great career
it's for the birds. cardinal flits to the feeder bar, perches edgy and adamant

depressing the recently recalibrated apparatus, pokes into the
     hole, eats, hops and the bar boings a bit, settles,
startles. doves are thugs. house sparrows, house finches, gold finches grip
     the droopy thistle bag
on the goldfinch feeder a red-tinged house finch who can't eat upside down
     like a goldfinch spins quick 360s, 6 o'clock peck 12 swallow, over
     and over (gravel)
eight months later William's son is back from serving in Iraq, hopefully like
     they say to stay
white cottontail look out, tail on the food-chain wagging the dog
arrested
hunkered in dusk, hops to the nearest prickly pear cover turkey vulture
hovering won't eat you
quick Cooper Hawk
long gone when the bough breaks the raptor will fall.
zen dream yoga. here in green fin leaf land the sun makes
half the surfaces translucent again, a little hopping breeze oddly doesn't
     make much difference in the irregular distribution of transfixed
     and opaque leaves, or parts of leaves
& the branches too catch light in thin blotched lines along brief spans of
     length, while the rest stay dark tan or matte, one branch
shuffles the pattern around as a calm darkens among water lights here we go
     again, which puzzled Kenneth
or so he pretended. I think he took it as auger of settling down toward death
     not
yet or
I did. My father in his gray topcoat hulked in front of the bus, angry and
     frail
refusing to move he'd rapped the door window while the bus was still
     stopped the driver wouldn't open Ornie gently moved him. After
     her grinding death a little chance to say
I will not fucking budge. I wouldn't either, sitting zazen in the grass at their
     graves, ignoring their importunities
that I fucking well cut it out

66

what on earth was this anyway

just earth

but really it was
calm with no darkening water lights just light and peaceful,
like the slow waving giant rushes maybe twenty feet tall glinting in that other
        light, spacious with that other death,
teeny kensho. One summer my father tagged along
to New Mexico after his boyhood anthropologist friend Morey Opler,
        brought back the tranquil beautiful manically geometrized Zuni
        pot I seem finally to have lost
Uncle Morey got caught at Cornell in the black student walkout brandished
        shotguns feeling miffed
"icy with pleasure"? whatever happened to that Diane with the Cathy with
        the why should this circuitous opaque filial stuff be my anticipatory
        mortality portion instead? some other restaurant nope. shuffling
        off this mortal coil indeed, dad's bus-fronting overcoat, so be it.
        alternate list
bushes and grasses: palo verde, bougainvillea, prickly pear, bottle brush,
        ocotillo, Arabian jasmine, oleander, brittle bush, bottle brush, tiny
        sparrow hops now across the upstairs patio at dawn
skinny middle-class white boy in English Dept bathroom says to cellphone
        yo what up
bougainvillea, rose bush, lemon tree (grafted on orange), rose bush,
        baby azalea, orange tree (grafted on lemon), lemon (grafted)
        acacia, orange (on lemon), texas ranger (dead), pink oleander,
        pomegranate, red oleander, something, same something again,
        red oleander, lady banksia climbing roses, geranium, star jasmine:
        I greet you
concerning mortalia
"I vow to walk on through"

coo coo ca choo

*

Botched Hangings in Iraq Speed Sectarianism

The botched hanging of **Saddam Hussein** and two lieutenants in **Iraq** by its Shiite-led government has helped to accelerate Sunni-Shiite sectarianism across an already fragile Middle East

The chaotic executions and the calm with which Mr. Hussein confronted the gallows and mocking Shiite guards have bolstered his image among many of his fellow Sunni Muslims.

But something else is happening too

"Raising the ugly face of Shiites, expanding Iranian influence in the region,"

Shiites, whom he called rejectionists worse than Jews or Christians

"By and large, rejectionists are the most evil sect of the nation and they have all the ingredients of the infidels,"

"Saddam Hussein was the one courageous man among Arab leaders," said Ibrahim Mustafa Ibrahim, a school janitor. "We saw how he was executed. We saw everything."

January 17, 2007

*

Poem Written at the Age of Sixty

Gull in the wind
           in the windy straits off Belle Isle?
nope just a house sparrow taxiing in to the tarmac
           pinions stretched taut for a perfect touchdown. peck, schmeck.
which was to be demonstrated. lunch break:
a glass of papaya juice and back to work:
During the periods when the US is not actually at war with Iraq, the American
           public does not buy books
Why, for example, is there S&M in "1945," Newt Gingrich's 1995 fantasia
           about the World War II? "She rolled onto him,". . . "and somehow
           was sitting athwart his chest . . . 'Tell me or I will make you do
           terrible things.'"

commodius vicus of recirculation

Let us turn to historians who have written monographs on the country.
Virtual reality, cyberspace, 'post-photography', surveillance satellites,
           'smart' bombs, CCTV, telivised 'reality' shows all feature amongst
           the concerns. Hence, there are observations on the necessary
           embedment of technology

Adorned in the perverse rings of slavery, Sheena must soon join her naked
           companions-in-misery, their backs and shoulders gleaming with
           sweat...and often striped by Ixandja's whip-of-five-tongues. The
           zip of leather; the drumbeat and shouted orders; the yelps of pain;
           the constant groaning clatter of oars; and the protesting jangle of
           chains, all combine in a hellish cacophony

*Here you will find breif information about the different stages of the Historical
development in Iraq, from the oldest known traces of the early human
populations in this part of the world until the recent days in a chronological
order.*

*I hope that this humble effort would help younger Iraqi generations
in diaspora to maintain a better knowledge about the History of their*

Homeland,

Brooks, George E. "Peanuts and Colonialism: Consequences of the Commercialization of Peanuts in West Africa, 1830-70." **Journal of African History** 1975 (16) 29-54.

My book is not about any specific region, but about imperialism per se. it looks at cross-country data to estimate the impact of colonialim on growth, industrialization, export orientation, and human capital. The book contains theory, history, taxonomy of sovereignty, and, finally, estimation exercises. It offers systematic refutation of the claims of free trade and the civilizing mission of colonialism

The whipped cream is on a high shelf, as I reach for it your jacket rises like a window shade to reveal my ripe round ass right there in the middle of aisle three.

the revolt in **Iraq** was suppressed by force.

In **Britain** a segment of public opinion wanted to **"get out of Mesopotamia"**

Faysal wanted the throne if it were offered to him by the **Iraqi people**.

Winston Churchill, then colonial secretary, promised to carry them out. He was advised by **T.E. Lawrence**,

You Tube Samantha Brown tries on bikinis and **spanks** herself!!

Now, Jeff. Iraq was invented eighty years ago, as I'm sure everyone in this room knows, by Winston Churchill and Gertrude Bell, on a Sunday afternoon in Cairo, and they made a mistake. They shouldn't have created the country, they should have let it go into the three provinces that it had been under the Ottomans. Today,

that option—letting there be a Kurdish north, a Sunni middle, and
a Shiite south

Cute blonde amateur getting **her** sexy **ass spanked**

is not possible.

the French improved public services and provided commercial stability
the native standard of living declined and precolonial social structures
    eroded.

China appeared on the way to territorial dismemberment and economic
    vassalage. Several provisions of these treaties caused long-standing
    bitterness and humiliation among the Chinese

Definition of The West:
. . . .These are the 22 Western States
. . . . that form the American West

Chalabi teamed up with American neoconservatives to sell the war as the
    cornerstone of an energetic new policy to bring democracy to the
    Middle East -- and after 9/11, as the crucial antidote to global
    terrorism. It was Chalabi who provided crucial intelligence on Iraqi
    weaponry to justify the invasion, almost all of which turned out to
    be false, and laid out a rosy scenario about the country's readiness
    for an American strike against Saddam that led the nation's leaders
    to predict -- and apparently even believe -- that they would be
    greeted as liberators.

Newt Gingrich 1945 A 'what if' novel about World War II, in which Hitler
    conquers Britain. Early drafts included some steamy sex scenes
    which were subsequently toned down Chapter 1 retains a romp
    with a "pouting sex kitten".

New Abu Ghraib Abuse Photos
CLICK ON IMAGE FOR BIGGER PICTURE

Spank Me Softly If you like the idea of spanking or being spanked, but don't
like the idea of the pain, then the **Spank Me Soft** is the ideal sex
toy ...

Saddam Hussein has reportedly told prosecutors that his decision to
massacre 180,000 Kurdish citizens of Iraq was both legal and
justified.

Historical perspective on **Wahabi** fundamentalism and the commonalities
with Judeo-Christian fundamentalism.

Wahabi Shrine Temple
Jackson, Mississippi, USA.
www.**wahabi**shrine.org/ - 1k

June 26, 2006

*

I resume the overstaid fraction. birds shuddering wings open dower the
ersatz birdbath.

The United States military said Friday that it was investigating whether
American soldiers had killed a family of four Iraqi civilians in March
in their home
Early reports indicate soldiers may have raped a woman, burned her body
and killed the woman's family in a "crime of opportunity,"
two soldiers from the same unit were abducted while guarding a traffic
control point in the town of Yusufiya, and were killed by insurgents.
Their mutilated bodies were found along a booby-trapped road,

a soldier felt compelled to report it after the discovery of the bodies of his kidnapped comrades,

Both lie in the so-called Triangle of Death, an area of extreme hazard along the Euphrates River valley that has become a cauldron of insurgents, criminal gangs and lawless tribes. It was a munitions production base for Saddam Hussein's government, and the home of senior Baath Party members, whose villas line the palm-fringed river banks.

whether Marines executed as many as 24 unarmed Iraqi civilians after a roadside bomb explosion killed a Marine. the American military put out a news release saying that 15 Iraqi civilians in the town had been killed by an insurgent bomb attack.

the Army charged four American soldiers suspected of killing three detainees in Iraq and then threatening another American soldier with death if he reported the shootings.

the Marine Corps said it had charged seven Marines and one Navy Corpsman with murder and kidnapping in the April killing of an Iraqi man in a village on the western outskirts of Baghdad. the assailants are accused of planting a Kalashnikov rifle and shovel near the body of the victim, to make him appear to be an insurgent, after shooting him in the face four times.

Tyger Tyger burning bright

Deaths of Iraqi civilians fell in June from previous months

At least 840 Iraqi civilians died in June, down from 1,100 in May

February, the month that hundreds of civilians were killed in sectarian bloodletting following the bombing of a sacred Shiite shrine.

At least 21 bodies were found across Iraq, many showing signs of torture. One was a boy in Baghdad between the ages of four and six who had been tortured and shot in the head,

President Vladimir Putin ordered Russian special services to hunt down and kill those responsible for the embassy workers' deaths.

In an Internet video posted Thursday night, Osama bin Laden praised Abu Musab al-Zarqawi, the Jordanian militant killed in an American air strike this month.

Mr. Bin Laden defended the copious bloodshed engineered by Mr. Zarqawi,
  saying that Mr. Zarqawi "had clear instructions to "make neutral
  those who wished to be neutral."
Mr. Bin Laden ordered the ruler of Jordan, King Abdullah II, to allow Mr.
  Zarqawi's remains to be buried in his hometown, Zarqa, Jordan.
Turning his back to the plate and moving to the wall at a dead run, Mr. Mays
  speared the ball as it was about to go into the stands. Shaking his
  head as he rounded second, Mr. Snider returned dejectedly to the
  Dodger dugout. The Polo Grounds erupted in prolonged cheers.
  San Francisco lay mute.

June 30, 2006

while the Biafran revolution pummeled the living shit out of the political
  theory of the postcolonial promulgated by the gin and grenadine
  tippling, pith-helmet sporting peer aspirant set at Harvard, far-
  flung howling wilderness client state of Oxbridge

that was then

neocon neocon all the way home

they let em run a fucking *country?*

I just make it up as I go along

January 18, 2007

*

time to re-read *The Ego and the Id*
in a kalpa of murderous rage
it starts inward I'll turn it outward it starts outward I'll turn it inward Freud
  couldn't decide

I can't make up your mind for you Sigmund

thank god for the star pointed leaves

& thanks to the light as well hurtling toward us at light speed no matter what
we're doing

sidling up toward it or turning our backs and running in terror

no difference

putting a village to death   indolently fucking or writing

swording up out of the big reservoir of gnawing your own foot off impulses

or whacking your neighbor's foot with an axe

my personal ratchets are in pretty good working order

they don't usually shunt stuff over onto the bigger gears

I snap at myself or my kids I haven't yet beheaded scads or sliced my own
arm off at the elbow

standing ass deep in snow impressing Bodhidharma I vow not to praise
myself at the expense of others also the contrapositive

I don't know much about engineering

or pretty much anything else except logopoeia the dance of the intellect
among words

a brainy balletic crowd pleaser

the crowd is extremely small

the chow mein was way too salty   nachtraglekeit

turn over you salty dog, there's "sexual" violence and sexual "violence"

that's all the difference between them and me said Lacan

she said they kept on truckin'

over to Cleveland to find a good top goodbye Columbus

true man without rank

congruent to Bataille's Parisian difficulty no one would do the bloody deed
though many proffered their Ruggles of Red Gap stuffed heads
(metropolitan slice job)

their little game O Mayan Letters   nachtraglekeit gone horribly wronig
that's wrong

"like likes to like like"

Freud liked cleave and cleave

diacritics he didn't believe in

cleave 1 and cleave 2
& get you in bed with this again
like D.T. Suzuki's mobius mu
we call it no
so when Freud's daughter's friend who was his rabbi's daughter said (in
        Manhattan) that in sexuality unless there's defusion of instinct
        the aggressive impulses are no longer aggressive 'cause they're
        "bound" (it's facing the wrong way again)
I thought ha ha that's like Robert Aitken saying Nanquan cutting the cat in
        two
isn't literal and isn't violent (tell it to the cat)
whereas Lionel Trilling said Freud wanted to maintain some gravitas in a
        floaty time
what's the sound of one hand?
"little bodhisattavas come and eat your rice" no shmetaphor
nobody can do it or everyone does it all the time
I do it
like fusing and defusing instinct
tying her up for fun or setting out early one morning intent on putting an
        entire village to death before lunch using poison gas
and this interweaving goes on and on
whomp
Leo Bersani wasn't the first one to say it
though he may have especially enjoyed getting down on all fours and saying
        it (get down and smell the powder Ferlinghetti)
sadism a backformation from masochism (just follow the money stupid)
sitting down till you achieve oneness with all beings
sitting down on all beings
your chair is my face said giovanni singleton oops
I mean your face is my chair
I love that
but what? we choose to preserve it more or less inviolate
until later this afternoon
frittering address circuits like jujubees or sparks of accordioned bullion

a little amoral frottage in the penumbra of the long war the suffering of the
        battered and wily and right now unspeakably violent people of Iraq
        and their American Indy 500 team sponsors, a pit crew if ever there
        was one, checkered flagging Bush Cup
Norman said we should all be in mourning
every moment
ergo get down and smell the powder yum henceforth
the star leaves brush green swordgrass feel and grains of light against my
        face
good morning I'm the middle body of the same thing, with a brick wall just
        far enough behind it to register
as reddish sand tone not much more
and a little vertical shaft of pale blue at the building's edge, bound on the
        other side by the vertical line of my window bricks
if I move my head just right
otherwise the whole sky vanishes

the world is all that is the case
till you reach out your arm through dark to lean against the wall and fall
instead into the entirety of night with a perspicuous jolt that makes your
        bell ring
like a distant temple gong
"it's big, it's dark, and he's in it"
scholar of one candle blown out
and the high wind thrashed the stars against the insides of the sleeping bag,
        echoic sky
then they drifted in currents on down
and smelled the powder
don't move if you move it will break you in two at the waist
get up & walk calmly with head erect your eye fixed on nothing
or tomatoes in the kindergarten garden
one hand
in the lap of a vast intelligence
but what about when it's a complete disaster, that's it

but I'm trying to keep its teeth off me
at least till after lunch   Kanzeon
& keep warm I hope you are too
& in the hopefully like they say enormous interim maybe we can lie down
	(David said we lie down doing time)
someone else said time to depart this comedy
not yet
get outta here with your teeth
we think we're alive and we'll be dead later but that's baloney
said Norman   save a ghost
& the bucket with the poppable bottom
is everywhere, definitely including the bed
and all over the case histories if attentively read
and in the mind of man
and in Iraq, where maybe
they have better things to think about and do, but maybe not
the nation is destroyed, rivers and mountains remain
I vow to hold that
you walk through the still morning before the bombs start and hold it too
they shot him in the face four times
they tortured the little boy and shot his face
they raped her and burned her body in front of her family, and then her
	family
& nothing to do
but fall down in praise and blessing, wherefrom
everything arises to be done.

U.S. OUT OF IRAQ is one.

June 30, 2006

*

I may not mean it literally. kind of a big retraction? they protect them from

falling
bricks, I guess. once the avalanche
of shit rocks bones and blood
falls down at your behest
on your non-neighbor's hitherto unoffending head

and it's all they've got
between brains and boulders, shit storm and scrotum
can you simply yank your shit-ass wall
away & walk away?
ten indian chiefs were sitting around a campfire. They said "Joe, tell us a
        story."
And this is the story Joe told.

June 30, 2006

        *

what about after the fifteenth of the month?

        *

What's the character for Tenney?
I wake and feel the fell of dark not day?
not this time it'll be light in what forty-five minutes now forms
in the world of form start waking around me, gapping
and stretching the mirror
starts buzzing again what is the shape and color of that heart
dunno. I do though: check sweater, rough brown cloth,
Jennie's face cracking in a big smile looking straight at me praise this world
        to the angel sometimes
tears are the form praise takes inside her cancer she said. that's all Santa Fe
        division, spacious, boingy, and calm.
Tucson predawn report: downtown lights twinkling and hopping around
        a little in their furtive dreams, splayed open, several yellow lights

as if morsing around maybe because of the foreground plate glass
window
in the Tenney mirror the alienation drops quickly into a weighty sadness, a
diffusing tenderness like an old familiar wound, then nothing at all,
even the what is that heart that still sees them in the dark dropped
drowsing
into the big no pool, revenge of the Soto black cave not terrible
back to the things themselves
--which makes a time gap, signal stratification
self sedimented & striated through being's dark mud
neo-futurist ur-buddhist late modernism hello
synthetic cubism (thanks Leslie) is calm
report from the land of the cave
splashed down into darkness making sloshes
till even what is resting in it dissolves . . .
WHAM! Tenney comes shooting up out of it into the world of forms
hey I greet you at the beginning of a great career
which nonetheless—nope, whomp
is the whole of it. you're tardy sleeping world,
get up! things drowse in the dark dance the dream tango a little bit longer
though,
rippling slowly waking mirror as little by little
they rouse and buzz
good thing the heart held them safely all night long
slow in the what is the color and form of that heart which sees them
my nameless kids
in their bedseds uh oh RAM gaps
I call him Bubba Rum Dum said his dad
farting happily along, Kyoto, North Dakota
snow fields breaking up seeping to achipelagos amid the high dry yellow
sharp grass
adagios
of islands o New York my prodigal argus thrusts up out of that too
original face self-replicates and glints

I love the Chrysler Building
an answer to the conundrum of the human, and why we offer this retreat to
the enlightenment of bushes and grasses, which seem to be doing
just fine on their own:
the human is what pecks (the sparrow hunts and pecks) at the keyboard
waiting for dawn to get with it
in a familiar mix of bliss and somewhat irritable anticipation
three dogs gapping and stretching too in their sleeps
what is the color and shape of that doggy heart (hard to stop typing goddy)
sees biscuits and chompable birds in the drowsy mirror buzzing it slowly
awake
tangled up limbs and the dark groin
falling back into the pool or shimmying hard up out of it, I praise the
--whatever, meaning all of it. "I wanted closure." well
cat given lion cut and anesthetized tooth extraction to boot, bedraggled and
happy mews at me
I'm the dream in the mirror he's trying to roist, or is it roust I guess, or
rouse—
which is it, Fred? I'm the cat he says, in cat
I dedicate the waking mirror 5:42 a.m. to the enlightenment of bushes,
grasses, and cats.
wham.

periplum.

November 3, 2006

*

WEBSTER, Texas -- Police and family members said a 10-year-old boy
who died by hanging himself from a bunk bed was apparently mimicking the
execution of former Iraqi leader Saddam Hussein.

Sergio Pelico was found dead Sunday in his apartment bedroom, said Webster police Lt. Tom Claunch. Pelico's mother told police he had previously watched a Spanish television station's news report on Saddam's death.

"It appears to be accidental," Claunch said. "Our gut reaction is that he was experimenting."

An autopsy of the fifth-grader's body was pending.

Julio Gustavo, Sergio's uncle, said the boy was a happy and curious child.

He said Sergio had watched TV news with another uncle on Saturday and asked the uncle about Saddam's death.

"His uncle told him it was because Saddam was real bad," Gustavo said. "He (Sergio) said, 'OK.' And that was it."

Sergio's mother, Sara Pelico DeLeon, was at work Sunday while Sergio and other children were under the care of an uncle, Gustavo said. One of the children found Sergio's body in his bedroom.

Police said the boy had tied a slipknot around his neck while on a bunk bed.

Police investigators learned that Sergio had been upset about not getting a Christmas gift from his father, but they don't believe the boy intentionally killed himself.

Clinical psychologist Edward Bischof, of California, said children Sergio's age mimic risky behaviors they see on TV -- such as wrestling or extreme sports -- without realizing the dangers. He said TV appeared to be the stimulant in Sergio's case.

"I would think maybe this kid is trying something that he thinks fun to act out without having the emotional and psychological maturity to think the thing through before he acts on it," Bischof said.

"I don't think he thought it was real," Gustavo said of Saddam's hanging. "They showed them putting the noose around his neck and everything. Why show that on TV?"

Sergio's father urged other parents to warn their children not to do what they see on TV. The parents said they believe the media outlets that chose to repeatedly air the video of Saddam's execution were irresponsible.

Family members held a memorial for the boy Wednesday in the apartment complex activity center.

The family is trying to put together enough money to send Sergio's body to Guatemala for burial.

A fund has been set up at Bank of America. Donations can made at any branch in the name of Sergio Pelico.

*

from pulses of spring
image and cry of hesitant fate
darkness of the body your flesh
fell unsubduable, beautiful companion

unearthly blood fell darkly
taken away
it gleamed
a terrible open door

unearthly dancer grieving
your blood entered
your early heart
a name I loved

like a flower
I entered it possessed

*

I sound my barbaric yawp
full fathom five
a muddy stick

resentful   selfish   gruff
irritated   whiny   aggrieved
myopic   mean spirited   petulant
passive aggressive   lazy   tunnel visioned
I peed in my dumptruck   indolent   which was in the closet
I liked it   aggrieved entitlement   the cat tears up the couch again
angry   cowardly   niggardly
I was proud of saying aggrieved entitlement bc it was a witty phrase   spiteful
        vain
abrupt   recalcitrant   a "solitary committer"
repetitive   inveterate   a jive dancer
withdrawn   defensive   "he's too pompious"
manic   the wolf, the snake, the hog not wanting   overly ebullient
boisterous   not wanting   get jiggy wid it
in me   shoved dish
the cheating word, the frivolous wish, not wanting
regnant   triage prone
I jumped on your whoopies   loud   not wanting the brussel sprouts
barbed   inherently vicious   when I like brussel sprouts
viscous   said this is this   coveting her in bed
but this is that   I mean I was lying alone in bed and I coveted her   just
        this
this   craven   heapish
but Dick Cheney is a total asshole I'm sorry   waspy   avoid the dung
triumphant   who can compadre   preening
I changed the sheets just in case
coy now   with Cathy   not really unspeakable things
she was twenty-four every night at the beach   where is she
San Francisco
what is the color and shape of that heart
completely gone

December 13, 2006

*

84

FORT DIX, N.J. – Six foreign-born Muslims were arrested and accused Tuesday of plotting to attack Fort Dix and slaughter scores of U.S. soldiers – a scheme the FBI says was foiled when the men asked a store clerk to copy a video of them firing assault weapons and screaming about jihad.

May 9, 2007

GAZA CITY, Gaza Strip – Hamas militants have enlisted a figure bearing a strong resemblance to Mickey Mouse to broadcast their message of Islamic domination and armed resistance to their most impressionable audience

May 9, 2007

*

what about after the fifteenth of the month?
unveil your ideas be ready to act on them?
you will never need to worry about a steady income nope
you will touch the hearts of many.

January 3, 2007

FORTUNE   Why do we sit?

ozone stalagmites?
early morning air
straining the udder of my heart for its withheld drip?
yep buoyed up by damp in the pre-dawn wash
adrift on the balcony
hello I'm the darkness below the navel humming cosmically along
I've got a big thing below the navel you barbarian interloper how do you
          know
hi Maggie quit nuzzling my face good morning wet dog snout
bird on the left coo of two

mourning doves distant on the right at one o'clock
more incoming caw at nine bong
distant temple bell your name is darkness
wet I fall into float
drifting down unmoving
as a calm darkens among water lights all the old time zen boys
Rimbaudian synaesthesiologists
tactus eruditus
time to palpate some sound
sliding your middle body hand up along incipient dawn and onto the
        mourning dove's breast
as the coo vibrates
the other name of this stillness
BOOM   what you do to me
be careful darkness what are you doing?
Maggie you've snapped suddenly alert, patrolling or trolling, growling
over the railing staring over the wall down through the dreaming wash
        where something's awake what she sees
isn't what you see, which is suddenly what Rousseau saw and splayed
        through the no longer exactly Keatsian wide quiet emanated with
        eerie patience:
big nearly symmetrical but skewed tree going WHOMP I'm the foreground
        saying I don't speak
I shimmer a little, my train is an immense stillness with very hungry tigers
        inside it
the green vine angering for life like Stevens said
point one you can float in it it buoys you up point two it can chomp you and
        "rend your flesh" at any moment
yours truly Henri Rousseau, aka Hakuin & Maitraya (attorneys at law)
tromping through life with a big EAT ME sign pinned to my back
ha ha
the sexual sense isn't the pertinent one right now Jack
that tribal hunter in the bush who said what he felt every morning was pure
        terror to which he said yup and could hence go out and hunt

sundry deadly things tea ceremony each morning as if it could be his
       last one day it was, cut down by an assassin's sword like Janet
       Rodney's grandfather, making the light shimmer like a Rousseau,
       how about: walk out the gate each morning wearing your eat me
       sign
there is no gate
talk that talk where does the evil of the year go?
blip thin air so it can hover as the beauty in Rousseau always ready to
       spring
and grind you to powder ignore it yes sir don't move if you move it will
       break you in two at the waist
ozone stalagmite September New York wind now palm to palm with spring
       has sprung
or what is the sound of one hand
in Tucson Arizona your face wafts out, soft cotton batting of the distant
       temple bell goes BONG
bong
bong

hears the clocks in the   *HUH?*
this is your country and the hour of love

yes space is tolling   canon hours
every single moment
ah

                                    March 25, 2007

*

Project Rebuild Iraq 2008
The 5th International Rebuild Iraq Exhibition

5 - 8 May 2008
Amman Exhibitions Park, Amman, Jordan

Project Rebuild Iraq 2008: The 5th International Rebuild Iraq Exhibition: Your Gateway to a Reconstruction market worth more than $100 Billion Dollars.

Project Rebuild Iraq 2008 is going to be a high-profile event showcasing one of the most ambitious, investment-opportunity-laden reconstruction undertakings of your era. It's going to be the biggest, most comprehensive Iraq reconstruction event ever held. If you are a construction sector player eyeing the Iraq reconstruction market, looking for a well-timed point of entry, seeking to gain maximum exposure and brand consolidation for your projects, or simply looking for potentially-rewarding business contacts, then Project Rebuild Iraq 2008 is the show for you. And if you're already active in Iraq's thriving reconstruction market, then Project Rebuild Iraq 2008 is going to immeasurably polish your profile.

Project Rebuild Iraq 2008 will set a new gold standard for Middle East exhibitions, drawing on the success of past IFP Group-organized Rebuild Iraq conferences. The show will be jointly organized by IFP Group, its Jordanian arm IFP Jordan, and the Riyadh Exhibitions Company. Over 25 years, they have organized more than 320 internationally-accredited trade shows across the Middle East.

As of 2008 'Rebuild Iraq' Rebrands to 'Project Rebuild Iraq' to Consolidate Position as the World's Leading Iraq Reconstruction Show

Since its inception in 2004, the 'Rebuild Iraq' exhibition has acquired a worldwide reputation as the world's pre-eminent Iraq reconstruction show. Over the years, other Iraq reconstruction shows with similar names have sprung up. As of next year, 'Rebuild Iraq' is re-branded as the Project Rebuild Iraq exhibition, to underscore its unique identity as the world's premier Iraq reconstruction exhibition, and to clearly differentiate it from other Iraq reconstruction shows.

Massive Market Opportunities in Iraq and Jordan at Project Rebuild Iraq 2008

Seize Unique Investment Opportunities Offered by Iraq's $100 Billion Reconstruction Market, and Jordan's Development Boom

Iraq's reconstruction market is worth a stunning $100 billion - making it one of the biggest anywhere in the world - and is set to expand further, as yet more contracts are signed and projects drawn up. Frenzied construction activity surrounds hundreds of projects, worth billions of dollars, and spanning every single sector of Iraq's rebounding economy. Iraq's liberal, open markets - almost entirely free of restrictions - are helping fuel construction sector activity. Meanwhile, ever more leading manufacturers and suppliers from across the globe are seizing lucrative slices of Iraq's construction market, and in doing so are helping positively forge the future of the country. Benefits from Iraq's construction sector are set to increase further. The country's revenue generation potential - bolstered by abundant oil and other resources, as well as the long-term commitment of global donors to the reconstruction effort - is enormous. It can rival all other major regional economies.

December 26, 2007

*

A POEM FOR WILLIAM'S SON

we've never met
I'm glad you're back
I'm glad you didn't die in Iraq

time to slow down
feel time unfurl
tic toc
I'm glad you didn't die in Iraq

I bet you saw some awful stuff
spawn of Bushian fluff

I pray for the enlightenment of bushes and grasses
but I'd really like to frag their self-righteous neocon asses

April 10, 2007

*

BONG indeed
bong
bong
bong

boing?
well sure
pluck yr magic twanger gambol quail
& yes they get busy scuttling about tweezing seeds again, why not?
Brownian motion, chapter umpteenth

everything plays stop the sound of the distant temple bell
my hands wrists biceps skull and inner head land of a thousand dances and
        gradually attenuating overtones
cactus wren chirrrrr crow caw mourning doves WHoooooo they're not so
        obviously thuggish right now & later inside parakeets still under
        their sheet chip chip chee WHOO chip chee
moral it looses moral it has never ceased to flow sycamore I see you have a
        woodpecker in yr hole enlightened consciousness
Latke slides near wanting to drift unobjectionably under my hand and
        push up stop shoving my wrist I'm typing lies back down licks and
        tooths at her right hind leg on the tile, assiduously licks front paw
my head has pretty much stopped vibrating
but my arms vibe the overtones, shoulders too
I know something else that's often a good instance of this we lie down
        doing time said David
swimming too or floating hippo-ish in the pool on the orange long tube
        spaghetti floaty bob bob bob
davening probably too like the bloke in the black hat & gabardine coat all
        night on the New York bound Tucson plane in the tight focus of
        his nightlight perusing the sacred
from the enclave around fifth street
the birdcalls get tiny & everything glides away from dawn now toward the
        business of day, variously intense tense funny lascivious slack
        cherubic or boinged
or else dawn rolls away like a stage set sliding behind or under it, disrobing
        the busier backdrop
russet mantle clad etc.
before it was I dunno like the immense rattle of a diffuse genius loci snake
        who meant no menace like Leslie says the comic book is calm
        because anyway everything was snake
not the feeling David had when stepping on the dark snake in Brazil in
        sandals he said it felt like a baggie containing shit then it kind
        of whirred then bit that round bump on the ankle bone I don't
        know what it's called like he said an electric drill, then flopped off

hard onto the dirt road and slithered off his leg then an intensely
    magnified stop that temple bell reverberator, receptacle or maybe
    powerstation
it didn't stop for days
he didn't die
but whenever it rains his leg gets whacked by the cosmic densho cop
hose slurs water into the mysteriously emptied spa
hard not to mean the attendant air of privilege which is actually a whole lot
    more minimal than it sounds
land of a thousand dependents
matte green scrub up the hills toward the serious mountain goes washier
    green in the slanting down light
but the oppresses like the heft of cathedral tunes has absconded
leaving you face to face with save a ghost
someplace on the other side the mountain is gleaming its gouche red
    rockface back at the sun, *Catalina Glintorama* being the proper
    term
hi
who I guess you ok gentle reader I initiate you into the diffusely bonging
    body
boinging into roadside rabbit poised down now scampering stealthily into
    the brush
now you're a cactus pad feeling your spines
because I said so
apparently it's allowed to be Whitmanian
it's all happening at the zoo
intense dark green of the well-watered lady banksia climbing rose
    devouring entire west-facing plate glass pseudo second story
    window you're blocking all my light
good morning   and it is
not the light to the south where a single bird heads north in a liquid hurry
    picking up altitude then sliding from view
I dedicate this morning business
to the people of Iraq

and to you whoever you are now I take your hand that you be my poem
bong
into the general only apparently intermittent vibration
bzzzzzzz zzzzz zzzzz
says other shore this shore for sure
GA!

May 1, 2007

*

GUANTANAMO BAY NAVAL BASE, Cuba – The chief of the U.S. military
said Sunday he favors closing the prison here as soon as possible because he
believes negative publicity worldwide about treatment of terrorist suspects
has been "pretty damaging" to the image of the United States.
"I'd like to see it shut down," Adm. Mike Mullen said
During a tour of Camp Six, which is a high-security facility holding about
     100 prisoners, Mullen got a firsthand look at some of the cells; one
     prisoner glared at Mullen through his narrow cell window as U.S.
     officers explained to the Joint Chiefs chairman how they maintain
     almost-constant watch over each prisoner.
Asked why he thinks Gitmo should be closed, and the prisoners perhaps
moved to U.S. soil, Mullen said, "More than anything else it's been the
image – how Gitmo has become around the world, in terms of representing
the United States."
"I believe that from the standpoint of how it reflects on us that it's been
pretty damaging," Mullen said, speaking in a small boat that ferried him to
and from the detention facilities across a glistening bay.

Mullen also walked through an almost-completed top-security courtroom
where the military expects to hold trials beginning this spring for the 14
"high-value" terror suspects who had previously been held at secret CIA
prisons abroad. He was told that audio of the proceedings might be piped to
locations in the United States where families of the Sept. 11 terror attacks,
and perhaps others, could hear them.

Mullen's predecessor, retired Air Force Gen. Richard Myers, is a defendant in a lawsuit by four British men who allege they were systematically tortured throughout their two years of detention at this remote outpost. On Friday a federal appeals court in Washington ruled against the four men.

The facility is on land leased from the Cuban government under terms of a long-term deal that predates the rule of President Fidel Castro.

and what you do with the prisoners when they come back (to the United States)," Gates said.

contending that U.S. laws do not apply there because Guantanamo is not part of the United States.

COMMENTS

- 💬 Post a Comment

This article does not have any comments associated with it

1/14/08

*

BIRDS (!)
5:14 AM
bursting with it   or bursting it
hard to get an adequate sense of that onto the page
well

CHEE   CHIP
            CHEE-AWW   wa wa wa

        chee-ah   chee-aw
                              (Tenney right here)
        inopportune page break in the typed draft oh well to resume
blit blit blit
                 ki-ri   ri-ri
etc.

bowl of one hand
filled with the puff or fluff of mourning dove
or quail trace, soft boing rippling the palm
then multipoint tickle of kinetic chip or peck
settling down nesting so the palms come up held out raised to roughly chest
          height as offering
to the bowl of the world
or anyway bowl of the Tucson basin or the part of it immediately below the
          mountain
mesquite and palo verdes, multifarious cacti, cushion wash sand, dawn air
          lifting breeze and are cushioned companionably by 'em
I don't have any idea what that means anymore
the apostrophe's descending backwards it's forbidden,
hidden
make this a short one?
dum dum dum

hiatus

it's probably not Buddhist to brandish the squirt bottle at the cat it slinks off
          you can keep typing
they're shooting the little boy's face again
I don't imagine him very clearly
I am peopling the sand of Iraq with the mind's prickly pears
and large sculptural shards of blasted steel and tin, occasional body parts
and a mosque with its minaret blown clean open
lifted up in the wash in one hand,

Iraq's on the other side of the river
my job is to put out its fire
save the document
I vow to save the document
now that I've turned off the porch light
Rozzie's an intense iridescent green which she puffs
preening or in edgy anger or to poop
aerating her blue head just slightly
the pinny leaves on the palo verdes are similarly lifted a little in the breeze
a kinetic simile
which also gets puffed out a little and floats
at least briefly will it save all beings
if I make my body soft
sure   bless all of it
including the very large Gila Monster waddling across the 35 mile per hour
        section of Territory Drive through the dark
luckily I saw it and braked to a standstill & sat
it levered itself criss-cross over the asphalt deathtrap
past the terrible spellchecker without incident or bodily harm yes
if you're careful you can probably lift it in your lifted hands
before it turns and chomps the bejeezus out of you then refuses to let go
till carted dangling to the ER & pried off using a trusty combo of medical
        skill and a graduating succession of dowels
isn't that how it is
David said the venomous snake he stepped on in the dark in Brazil felt like
        a plastic bag full of shit, and then a pneumatic drill, then a spinal
        cordal flop then it slithered off
there are two Davids
his leg still hurts when it's damp
this is a long way from the birds
or it's not
my body is buoyed up by air I offer it raised in my two hands
this is totally wacko?
the orangy pink Gila Monster's beads I offer them too   here

hello air

the bird said David you're wrong

May 12, 2007

*

"The CIA's destruction of these tapes shows complete disdain for the rule of law. This reeks of a deliberate cover up of potential criminal activity by the CIA, and the videos could have shown once and for all that the CIA does indeed torture," said Anthony D. Romero, Executive Director of the ACLU.

CIA officials claim the tapes were destroyed partly out of concern that showing the brutal interrogation methods could expose the agency to legal risks.

the same day that Senator Dianne Feinstein (D-CA) added an amendment to the 2008 intelligence authorization bill that applies the Army Field Manual to all government agencies, including the CIA. The Army Field Manual prohibits specific acts of torture and abuse, including waterboarding,

Gee, whatever happened to being "innocent until proven guilty"? Or does that only apply to terrorists and other enemies of the US?

By the way what is the "crime" that is supposed to have occurred here anyway?

Whatever "waterboarding" is, it was not a crime at the time, and indeed, it is not a crime today.

But such details matter not one whit to the ACLU. They are simply America-hating liars.

The ACLU's only purpose <u>from its inception</u> has been the destruction of this country. Their hatred of our nation has always informed their every act.

And on that subject, can you think of anything more ironic than the ACLU's current slogan: "Because Freedom Can't Protect Itself."

When it's the ACLU that does everything it can to keep the US from protecting its freedoms.

1/14/08

*

why weren't you Tenney?
I was Tenney
YIPPEE! I'm glad I'm alive
"'I'm glad you're alive too, baby, because I want to fuck you'"
we're alive and we're dead
"we think we're alive now and we'll be dead later but that's baloney"
the idiom of American zen is the idiom of American poetry
SAVE A GHOST   in 48 point Houdini-JA type
we're swimming through the bardos, paddling around the shallow water
        part
amid the oscillating mats of light
it's not funny
the tree over there is a ghost waving its branches hi I can save them
all no this is the tree all them people over there including Tenney
Nathanson Associate Professor of   huh   I'm autocorrect my friend is your
        friend the spellchecker without rank glug glug glug save a ghost
        doesn't want to horse around right now
so it bathes your cement head
in cement, and water and wind and light
drifting through now from the other stars
swell that it's rhizomatic
my mother is a ghost she saves ghost Tenney
a hungry ghost doesn't know it's a ghost so it's hungry
is that right? so you feed it

its ghostness and it morphs along the rows of oscillating current they look a
        little like rotating lit up doormats
KATSU don't yell at the poor ghosts please they have it hard enough being
        gay and straight and ghostly
Please Don't Feed the Ghosts
quadrilingual sign on the French National Railway prohibited it said you can
        safely ignore
in Italian it said it's *dangerous* to stick your head out the window ha ha
Tim ghost Charles ghost Barb ghost Frank ghost
corporate poetry pog ghost fictive person where can any dust alight ghost
family correctly not enumerated by name all ghosts
Bobby Thompson ghost, souvenir ball ghost Don DeLillo brilliant chapter
        ghost
J Edgar Hoover ghost, Siri and Paul in Brooklyn ghost
John Ashbery's *Vermont Notebook* ghost
air ghost wind ghost the testicles and scrotal sac ghost yes wind whose soft
        whispering genitals tickle against me ghost scruffy Walt ghost
        canny Emily ghost Walt canny too
my beautiful doggie ghost, my live doggie and my dead doggie
Allen Ginsberg sightless in Moloch ghost enlightenment ghost enlightened
        one falls into a well ghost
climbs back out ghost
quit that
where do we find ourselves? along a huge prospect overlooking the Pima
        County Landfill
plastic bag shreds blow happily along, a huge snake
slithers across the sky and the Tucson basin shudders
no it's the snake that shudders no the mind
the mind doesn't shake
but it does Mickey's Monkey Mind, lumdy lumdy lie, lumdy lumdy lie-eye
I have no idea how to spell it wallowing along the oral tradition bardo the
        grizzled spellchecker lies down in total despair and dies
but not before correcting "grissled" the old fart
I don't know if I can let my ghostly dead drift slowly through my ghost body

four months later why not
yes mudmind alright frankly "I'm assuming that everything is alright and
        difficult"
but is snow falling in that other place? O
I am a ghost, and where I am
The Ghost Snow falls, and drifts
at a 30 degree angle horizontally through air
which isn't there
unless I say so
though being a ghost now
standing in ghost snow
what I say
drifts down like snow
that isn't there, dissolved
in air
not there
but IN you is the—huh?
when all the stars are mute
Yasutani as to destruction everything is destroyed as to no nothing is
        destroyed
which leaves you today's air, that means me, the ghost formerly known as
        Tenney thump thump thump
orange brick wall very bright now
huge pinon waving energetically in the stiff breeze maybe even agitated
are you ok tree? remember you're a ghost
just this this
I'll dance with all your needles brushing my face at the ghost ball
pale washed blue behind all of it gouached by light stumping the checker
and behind that the shoji screens
eternal bric a brac of the spotless mind
omnipresent like Big Mind
which is also a ghost
a big one

June 25, 2007 & January 14, 2008

*

blood in the saddle
here's my rendition of ghost riders in the sky
followed by the ghost's rendition of our national airborne rendition rider
I am he who signed three hundred and forty seven signing statements
I am he whose figure is outdated
when I say enlightenment I mean putting your head in a bag secured with a
   bowline
guess which chief executive gets to yank your chain
sometimes the music was American rap, sometimes Arab folksongs
Under torture after his rendition to Egypt, al Libi had provided a confession
   of how Saddam Hussein had been training al Qaeda in chemical
   weapons. This evidence was used by Colin Powell at the United
   Nations a year earlier (February 2003) to justify the war in Iraq.
   "Fortunately, this operative is now detained, and he has told his
   story.")
In this secret facility known to prisoners as "The Hangar" and believed to
   be at Bagram Air Base north of Kabul, al Libi told fellow "ghost
   prisoners" an incredible story of his treatment over the previous
   two years:
A Feb. 5 cable records that al Libi was told by a "foreign government
   service" (Egypt) that: "the next topic was al-Qa'ida's connections
   with Iraq...This was a subject about which he said he knew nothing
   and had difficulty even coming up with a story."
Al Libi indicated that his interrogators did not like his responses
Meanwhile, al Libi, who told fellow prisoners in Bagram he was returned
   to U.S. custody from Egypt on Nov. 22, 2003, has disappeared.
   He was not among the "high-value prisoners" transferred to
   Guantanamo last year.
I owned a lot of oil and the Texas Rangers
I am free
I lost a lot of money
I found religion I think I got saved
I found politics
I knew nothing and had difficulty even coming up with this story

the poem interrogates me it does not like my responses

I piss on its head like a true blueblood

I have quietly claimed the authority to disobey more than 750 laws enacted
        since I took office, asserting that I have the power to set aside any
        statute passed by Congress when it conflicts with my interpretation
        of the Constitution.

Legal scholars say the scope and aggression of my assertions that I can bypass laws represent a concerted effort to expand my power at the expense of Congress, upsetting the balance between the branches of government. The Constitution is clear in assigning to Congress the power to write the laws and to the president a duty "to take care that the laws be faithfully executed." I, however, have repeatedly declared that I do not need to "execute" a law I believe is unconstitutional.

Former administration officials contend that just because I reserve the right to disobey a law does not mean I am not enforcing it: In many cases, I am simply asserting my belief that a certain requirement encroaches on presidential power.

But with the disclosure of my domestic spying program, in which I ignored a law requiring warrants to tap the phones of Americans, many legal specialists say I am hardly reluctant to bypass laws I believe I have the constitutional authority to override.

Examples of the president's signing statements
GLOBE GRAPHIC: **Number of new statutes challenged**

Far more than any predecessor, I have been aggressive about declaring my right to ignore vast swaths of laws -- many of which I say infringe on power I believe the Constitution assigns to me alone as the head of the executive branch or the commander in chief of the military.

For the first five years of my presidency, my legal claims attracted little attention in Congress or the media. Then, twice in recent months, I drew scrutiny after challenging new laws: a torture ban and a requirement that I give detailed reports to Congress about how I am using the Patriot Act.

For examples of my signing statements **click here**.

The president, as commander in chief, can waive the torture ban if he decides that harsh interrogation techniques will assist in preventing terrorist attacks.

Only the president, as commander in chief, can place restrictions on the use of US armed forces, so the executive branch will construe the law "as advisory in nature."

All military attorneys are bound to follow legal conclusions reached by the administration's lawyers in the Justice Department and the Pentagon when giving advice to their commanders.

The inspector general "shall refrain" from investigating anything involving sensitive plans, intelligence, national security, or anything already being investigated by the Pentagon. The inspector cannot tell Congress anything if the president decides that disclosing the information would impair foreign relations, national security, or executive branch operations.

I am the country's first MBA President.

May 13, 2008

I'm sitting astride a time warp.
Philip Whalen said there's a wonderful kind of poetry that's written right
        now that's not written now
or something like that I asked Leslie and Norman to explain it to me
I think it's what I'm doing
at this point in the poem we're mired deep in the roiling crap and sodden
        stench of the Bush presidency
out there beyond the window Barack Obama's been elected
I should have written faster
it seems a little mean spirited to shake my fist at the first black president

elect for putting my poem in a tight spot, or pretend we're still in
       Bushville out of a pugnacious regard for the unities
it's cloudy today, the air is soft and though it's Arizona full of floating water
       my name is Ocean Blossom (blam!)
it was amazing on election night to see the black new extended first family
       get up on stage including one teenage kid in cornrows
what's the country coming to
well for one thing it's teetering on the brink of another great depression
       though everyone says that's not possible
what about after the fifteenth of the month
when it's a disaster
my country 'tis of thee
the rabbit and the beercan have disappeared
a gap making the air softer

Than Oars divide the Ocean,
Too silver for a seam—

I'm not sure where the dashes go
or the butterflies, or banks of flowers at noon
is that what it means
they have all gone into the   what?

where does the evil of the year go O'Hara asked
in beautiful September New York air, October too actually
especially at night bizarre being teary twenty-seven years later
hey Tenney where does the evil of the year go
last night your head hummed into the buzzing light
transcendentalized pumpkin brimming the floaty ether
which now are we in here huh Barack Obama I greet you at the beginning of
       a great career
Barack=Walt? quod erat demonstrandum?
I shake my white locks at the runaway sun

the body of Walt is the body politic after all I'm sorry I doubted it run through
          the body of the Buddha
all three bodies   tomorrow see you probably in Nirmanakayaland bump
          bump BLAM
but today is national Sambhogakaya day thank you dear clouds making
          oatmeal in the Alps with me I walked right through your middle
          body headlights loomed into view at about six feet dangerous and
          dreamy
bless the President of the United States of America startling to say it and it's
          not a cheap shot
and mossy scabs of the worm fence, and heaped stones, and elder and
          mullein and pokeweed
the spellchecker poked it, the carceral's back there somewhere biding
          its time and chiseling slightly into Whalen's now, otherwise
          attractively porous
how come you can say anything next
for example: I proclaim the advent of National Dharmakaya Day WHAM
          everything jolted into existence except all the stuff slid down into
          nonexistence blub blub into the cloudfog illuminated momentarily
          by headlights around hairpins
so it can stand here firmly rooted and float

same gigantic pine tree wagging a little in the wind
maybe eighty feet high? and my two rows of bushes down around the
          building's edge out of sight
are not in the now? soft bubbly ones little pointy ones
examples of Uji which I don't understand
a little coloquey the spellchecker completely flabbergasted
oh colloquy, bathed in flora's eros, another now laved in floaty light
it's National Floaty Light Day, National I get to lave you now Walt said
          "undrape!"
praise the   whatever

the poem contemplates its nows like Emerson's two horses in "Fate"
watch out for the hooves jumping poet

for a moment they threaten to converge, merge into the hobgoblin of little
        portfolios
uh uh
not addicted to a foolish consistency
O orange brick wall you come to my aid looming up behind the complementary
        soft green of the tree needles with a pleasing thwack

am I allowed to say it   What is the true Dharma eye

November 25, 2008

*

50 Result(s) for squirrel

The Lucky *Squirrel* Scratcher/ My Lucky Lottery Charm coin. .... Pest
Control, commercial

carpet beetle removal, bird control, ants,

Tell you students that now they are going to be poets. Take them outside and give each student a copy
of the *Write a Poem!* handout. Have them observe a living thing: a squirrel, a beetle, ants, etc – just
preferably not a bird. As they watch their object, have them fill out the handout. . . . The second part of
the worksheet asks them to make a web cluster for their new object. By the end of the activity, students
should be able to create a very brief story for their animal.

They looked like frightened
Beads, I thought–

Continue to the second and third lines, working your way through the poem. Encourage the students to discover what is happening in each line and to think about what they already know about how birds act. The last two stanzas will be most difficult for them. Help them to see how Dickinson compares the sky to an ocean. Remind them of what they learned about metaphors. For example, with "Too silver for a seam," students could focus on showing something "silver" or shining

Now, read the poem again with your students and ask them how Dickinson describes a bird. Does Dickinson describe some of the same qualities they saw in the images and found through the brainstorming activity?

Can you visualize the act of rowing?

*

There are regions
that seem like seas
all our possible
breathing   single wave

winds invisible places
inside me.
Are the wandering
air and space

rhythmically counterweight regions in
wave motion, leaf and smooth bark absorbed in
gradual seas? Interchange, you
invisible world grown

possible,
recognize me.

2.1, 7/1/09

*

Pakistan suicide bombing kills 23 in 'Taliban revenge attack'

Terrorists struck against Pakistan's security forces with devastating effect, killing at least 23 people in a suicide car bombing in Lahore.

May 27, 2009

*

"I really do believe that we will be greeted as liberators. I've talked with a lot of Iraqis in the last several months myself, had them to the White House. The president and I have met with them, various groups and individuals, And like Kanan Makiya who's a professor at Brandeis, but an Iraqi, he's written great books about the subject, knows the country intimately, The read we get on the people of Iraq is there is no question but what they want to the get rid of Saddam Hussein and they will welcome as liberators the United States when we come to do that." (Cheney, *Meet the Press*, 3/16/03)

"I think that the people of Iraq would welcome the U.S. force as liberators; they would not see us as oppressors, by any means. And our experience was after the Gulf War in '91 that once the United States acted and provide leadership that in fact, the community, the region was more peaceful for some considerable period of time. That is what made possible a lot of progress in peace process between the Israelis and Palestinians back in the early '90s." (Cheney, *CNN American Morning*, 9/9/02)

"Think of the faces in Afghanistan when the people were liberated, when they moved out in the streets and they started singing and flying kites and women went to school and people were able to function and other countries were able to start interacting with them. That's what would happen in Iraq." (Rumsfeld, Media Roundtable, 9/13/02)

"The Iraqi people understand what this crisis is about. Like the people of France in the 1940s, they view us as their hoped-for liberator. Our plan, as President Bush has said, is to remain as long as necessary, and not one day more. " (Wolfowitz, Remarks to VFW conference, 3/11/03)

[Rejecting Army Secretary Eric Shinseki's assessment that the mission would require large numbers of troops for a long duration:] "We can't be sure that the Iraqi people will welcome us as liberators, although based on what Iraqi-Americans told me in Detroit a week ago, many of them - most of them with families in Iraq - I am reasonably certain that they will greet us as liberators, and that will help us to keep requirements down. In short, we don't know what the requirement will be, but we can say with reasonable confidence that the notion of hundreds of thousands of American troops is way off the mark." (Wolfowitz, House Budget Committee, 2/27/03)

"I hope we would be seen as liberators. I think that might well be the case. " (Powell, *Meet the Press*, 2/9/03)

"We understand the implications of such a change of regime action and have made a commitment, to ourselves, anyway, as we start down this road that we would have obligations to see it through. We would hope that if it came to that, there would be such a sea change in the region, rather than it being seen as an assault, it would be seen as a liberation, as Mr. Lantos has spoken of. " (Powell, HIRC, 9/19/02)

"The point, again, to be - to work with our international coalition, to work through the U.N., to work through our military, to make certain that there is stability in the region. And take a look at what's happening in Afghanistan now, And the people of Afghanistan view the United States as liberators... Now that's not to predict what the ultimate outcome could be if we go to war, because nobody is saying a war will not have difficulties and there would not be casualties. My point is, the likelihood is much more like Afghanistan, where the people who live right now under a brutal dictator will view America as liberators, not conquerors." (Fleischer, Press Briefing, 10/11/02)

"I think the Iraqi people would welcome freedom with jubilation." (Andrew Card, *Fox News Sunday*, 1/26/03)

12/1/08

*

O tree formerly known as save a ghost
today you're make the mountains dance
the window is the same
down below a student slinks by lugging a huge skateboard
WS Merwin can't spell
He said Loren Goodman was like a debutante on a skateboard
Jon Anderson said Merwin thinks Loren is a girl now he's dead
the ghost tree drapes its branches in cool light and flicks them back and
        forth just a little in flecks of wind
so the mountains dance
the cold noodles are spicier and a girl swings her crossed right leg back and
        forth too nervously fast
one of the candidates for chair of the RNC sent around a Christmas card
        with a funny song called Barack the Magic Negro ha ha
last week at the Little Chapel Barb, Roberto, Jen, and Tenney sat still in the
        hall like mountains dancing
tiny rivulets coursed down us birds started up from unimagined coverts
in the lineage of Norman said yeah right it's no different from Keats but what
        it offers is a method
not madness
where the bush is make the mountains dance and the rocks & cracked and
        patched asphalt
Barack Obama sits in the winter light waiting to be ensconced
George Bush sits in Crawford Texas making the mountains dance
this is the greater vehicle
mountain ghost Bush ghost wind ghost Merwin ghost poor Jon Anderson
        ghost
where did they bury the giant tv
o pinon the wind is making you very agitated right now don't worry
you win the koan contest show me an immovable tree in a heavy wind
truth also has its paleontology
down there under the ground and in the cortical layers right above it you
        scarcely move

as to destruction everything is destroyed as to no nothing
hop hop hop lots of good time and energy being the windy part
yelling AAAAA at the void the multifoliate living junk in the foreground
the spellchecker says it doesn't exist once it said asshole not found
the big mountain up past the tree like WCW's young sycamore
a crenellated rhythm caught in freeze-frame
Keats's kinetic trace past participles EP/FEN said everything leaking
    motion
if the mountain weren't dancing already how could I make it dance
it's not dancing stupid
that's true too
it's raining and it's not raining
no no there said Freud
dark beautiful rainclouds of the mind dance with the actual sky's bright
    windy blue that's the January dance
o rain on the roof unheard
and always elegiac on second avenue
the sound of the rain on tin
into the unwilling sea, that's right
the bottom drops out of the Rinzai bucket floating in abstraction though the
    huge dark sky
rendering light I typed rending let them dance
the mountain dances rending the light
when the crenellations get busy the birds jump
and the butterflies cascade around the bushes the brittle bush and bottle
    brush
Paul jumps in Texas too hearing crenellated again
it's getting busy
dancing ghost crenellated ghost wind ghost
which is not falling in that other place
and the sudden snow on the ground the last morning was so beautiful I could
    only put my palms together and walk in the line weeping with my
    hands in gassho now we call it greeting
o fuddled spellchecker be still

no it's the spellchecker that moves said Hui Neng no a later teacher said the
    spellchecker doesn't move
behind it still the immense dancing blue
o sky I hum you on your way   hereby
yep below the heavens and above the earth world honored one

January 15, 2009

Hamdan v. Rumsfeld, **548 U.S. 557** (2006) The case considered whether
    the **United States Congress** may pass legislation preventing the
    Supreme Court from hearing the case of an accused combatant
    before his military commission takes place, whether the special
    military commissions that had been set up violated federal law
    (including the **Uniform Code of Military Justice** and treaty
    obligations), and whether courts can enforce the articles of the
    1949 **Geneva Convention**.
On June 29, 2006, the Court issued a 5-3 decision holding that it had
    jurisdiction, that the administration did not have authority to set
    up these particular military commissions without congressional
    authorization, because they did not comply with the **Uniform
    Code of Military Justice** and the Geneva Convention (which the
    court found to be incorporated into the Uniform Code of Military
    Justice).
Just days earlier, Hamdan's defense attorney Lieutenant Commander
    Charles Swift had been named one of the 100 most influential
    lawyers in America by the National Law Journal. But in October,
    the Navy announced plans to dismiss him under its **"up or out"**
    promotion policy.
An unusual aspect of the case was an **amicus brief** filed by Senators **Jon
    Kyl** (R-Ariz.) and **Lindsey Graham** (R-S.C.), which presented
    an "extensive colloquy" added to the Congressional record as
    evidence that "Congress was aware" that the **Detainee Treatment
    Act of 2005** would strip the Supreme Court of jurisdiction to

hear cases brought by the **Guantanamo** detainees. Because these statements were not actually included in the December 21 debate, **Emily Bazelon** of *Slate magazine* has argued this was an attempt to mislead the court.

1.4 million on the mall
"I'm not fearing any man"

airborne rendition
sedition
unitary executive
expletive

swing low sweet chariot

O helicopter I have been most glad to see whirl off in all my life
send him home
send him home
send him home

January 22, 2009

*

"The nation is destroyed. Rivers and mountains remain."

don't exaggerate

This Is No Time to Think Small

a world at every plunge

and finished knowing—then
surprise
 it's the land of the infinite popup

sproinging not springing you idiot
into existence American late late capitalism new improved iteration of
      cosmic pinball
deaf dumb blind   let's run up the score
self criticism yes I can see myself too as a Ponzi scheme I can buy
      into it

rivers are destroyed (regional art)   mountains remain

where do we find ourselves
receding clouds like tossed aside layers of overlapped cotton batting
or balls, to which someone applied a light gouache
bright red oleander foreground likewise a little sponged
palm behind them ebulliently still and, where prior owner had lower branches
      pruned, a patchwork of plate tectonics   Whitman's alligator ("in
      his tough pimples")
I peck about the gravel
he said pick actually peck makes the kinetic echo sharper pick is probably
      more accurate when it comes to sparrows
sparrow says cheep cheep crow says caw caw he said   one hand
oops it's a secret
"as to destruction everything is destroyed as to no nothing"
prodigiously wise
anti-semitic asshole
it's all tessellated
what's the sound of one hand when you're dying
palest blue peeks through the batting
currently incarnate particular sparrows cheep in the yard
a/c kicks itself into life TEP says 5 lemons pay up
the bank buildings huddle way off there tucked under the mountains`
shoulder to shoulder but smaller
yep regional art
the what is it now maybe Wells Fargo Building? a light matte desert brown
      actually really beautiful

earth drowsing dawn in the monsoon the close trees and bushes outside the
        wall bubbling up leaves in their dreams drifting down to the wash
what is this koan
do you believe in reincarnation   how many steps does it take to get to this
        room   and original face
and the kids tumbling through it
not a pinball machine a clothes dryer built by Claus Oldenberg

"what is this happiness"

ping

P'ang Rilke said

"life is always right"

This is the robe of freedom
the bare field
the blessings

July 24, 2009

*

Precision Timepiece by Ernst Block and Associates

list your most important qualification for this job: I have an MBA

also I'm like a Legacy Carrier   one checked bag one carry-on not to exceed
        dimensions two billion contrailing gallons red ink
come to think of it I am a Legacy Carrier

July 24, 2009

THE SHADOW BANKING SYSTEM

The **shadow banking system** or the **shadow financial system** consists of **non-bank financial institutions** that, like banks, borrow short, and in liquid forms, and lend or invest long in less liquid assets[1]. They are able to do this via the use of **credit derivative** instruments which allow them to evade normal banking regulations, e.g. those related to specifying ratios of **capital reserves** to debt. Many "shadow bank" like institutions and vehicles have emerged in American and European markets, between the years 2000 and 2008, and have come to play an important role in providing credit across the global financial system.[2]

The system includes **SIVs, conduits, money funds, monolines, investment banks, hedge funds** and other non-bank financial institutions. These institutions are subject to market risk, **credit risk** and especially **liquidity risk**, since their liabilities are short-term while their assets are more long term and illiquid. This creates a potential problem in that they are not depositary institutions and do not have direct or indirect access to their central bank's lender-of-last-resort support. Therefore, during periods of market illiquidity, they could go bankrupt if unable to refinance their short-term liabilities.[3]

Until the summer of 2007, **structured investment vehicles** (SIVs) and **collateralised debt obligations** (CDOs) attracted little outside attention and were not always fully recognized on the **balance sheets** of their affiliated banks. Since then the shadow banking system has been blamed[2] for aggravating the **subprime mortgage crisis** and helping to transform it into a global **credit crunch**.[4]

Examples

- **Bear Stearns** Collapsed in March 2008 due to funding

issues, and rescued by Fed-brokered and -backed deal with JP Morgan, which purchased the firm at $10/share with Federal guarantees against potential future CDO losses.

- **Lehman Brothers Holdings** (Filed for bankruptcy on September 15, 2008)

a mortgage lender makes a loan to a homeowner and then gets the loan out of the bank by selling a security interest in it like a stock, people being able to buy a stock interest in a bundle of mortgages, and that's called the securitization process. Because of the sub-prime nature of this people were not anxious to buy this stock because you're essentially buying a stock in somebody's ability who doesn't have credit to pay their mortgage. So they sliced and diced these mortgage backed securities into something called collateralized debt obligations, which simply made a bigger range of mortgage backed securities, nationalized them so you weren't buying into a single region of the country, and then listed them in what are called tranches, or levels of risk associated [I see, I see]. Unfortunately the most senior tranche was given a credit rating by credit rating agencies of triple A which is a whole nother question we can deal about. But then the shadow market most importantly comes in two forms. One, people ran out of mortgages for people to have an interest in, and investors were so interested in getting into this wonderful market, they created synthetic collateralized debt obligations, which essentially are like fantasy baseball. You don't own Alex Rodriguez but you get together with a group of people and you pick Alex Rodriguez as your player and to the extent he succeeds you succeed. What happened here was people bought mimicked collateralized debt obligations, the parts of it that were triple A rated. In other words the extent the real collateralized debt obligations succeeded, theoretically they succeeded. There were many more of these synthetics than there were real, so you're magnifying the risk; that is to say, Alex Rodriguez doesn't only lose the ball game, but a lot of people are out there in the economy in this case the equivalent of investing in Alex Rodriguez.

(Diane Rehm show)
Feb 27-March 3, 2009

Tenney wants to add: one thing AIG did was jump heavily into insuring these collateralized debt instruments through credit default swaps and also naked credit default swaps—that's the fantasy baseball part: you buy a tranche in a mimicked collateralized debt obligation, you own an interest, that is, in a mortgage not defaulting though you have no actual financial connection to the actual mortgage, and I'm AIG and I insure you against the possibility that the guy whose house is mortgaged and the mortgage is held by some bank, say Citigroup, defaults on his loan, and he does default, and although you were just in the fantasy baseball part of this you had bought one of these derivatives for real money and now that the guy can't pay his mortgage and it's part of a big tranche where a lot of guys suddenly can't pay their mortgages, and so this derivative that you paid a lot of money for is suddenly not worth much, and you're screwed. But hold on: I'm AIG and I've insured Citigroup against a decline in the value of the tranche they bought, so I pay Citigroup a nice chunk of change, but I've also insured your fantasy baseball ownership of the virtual tranche, and so I pay you a nice chunk of change bc some guy in Bethesda defaulted on his mortgage even though you don't by any stretch of the imagination own any piece of his actual mortgage, you just own a fantasy extension derivative, that's the naked part, and so I pay you. And who pays me? The federal bailout, the taxpayers, whose money given to AIG goes in the front door and out the back door, to, say, Citigroup at 100 cents on the dollar (no one required Citigroup or anyone else to take a write-down) and it also goes out the door to you, the guy who owned the fantasy baseball interest in Alex Rodriguez's mortgage, I mean the fantasy mortgage that's like the fantasy Alex Rodriguez. But wait there's more. Because there's this other guy: unlike you he didn't buy a fantasy interest in a mortgage he didn't own, because while you thought the guy in Bethesda would pay his mortgage and your AIG insurance policy was just hedging, I'm betting heavily that the housing market's all coked up and a lot of guys in a lot of Bethesdas won't be able to keep up with their mortgage payments for very long, and their mortgages will tank. So I don't buy a fantasy Alex Rodriguez mortgage I just buy a lot of insurance as if I had. I go to AIG, and buy an exorbitant amount of insurance against the disaster of some possibility I don't have any literal financial stake in, whether direct or naked: I take out a million dollar insurance policy against the possibility that poor Joe in Bethesda, or stupid greedy Joe in Miami, can't make the payments on his million dollar condo, even though I won't sustain any financial loss if he fails to keep up, I don't own a real or a fantasy tranche even in Alex's house, I steered clear. So I go along making my monthly insurance payments to AIG for a couple years and shit, Joe in Bethesda defaults, and I collect a million dollars. It's like taking out insurance against your house burning down even though I don't own your house, you do, or your naked house. Might I then have an interest in, omigod, your house burning down?

I'm not making this stuff up.

March 19, 2009

2.4

gleaming the
mirror hollowed
out looking
inside seen

calmly once
need didn't
nourish purity
space appeared

not the
same love
but movements
white animal

eyes never
mere being

July 30, 2009

WASHINGTON –The Justice Department released **a long-secret report** Monday chronicling abuses inside the **Central Intelligence Agency**'s overseas prisons, showing how interrogators choked a prisoner repeatedly and threatened to kill another detainee's children.

Skip to next paragraph

Michael McAndrews/Hartford Courant

John H. Durham, a veteran Connecticut prosecutor, has been investigating the C.I.A.

In response to the findings, Attorney General **Eric H Holder Jr.** chose John H. Durham, a veteran prosecutor from Connecticut who has been investigating the C.I.A.'s destruction of **interrogation videotapes**, to determine whether a full criminal investigation of the conduct of agency employees or contractors was warranted. The review will be the most politically explosive inquiry since Mr. Holder took over the Justice Department in February.

Tiger Company

Tiger Company Guarantee

Tiger-Sul Products takes pride in being a full service company. Over the past several years Tiger-Sul has taken steps in making our offer to you, our valued customer, even better.
A Quality Assurance Program is in place to maximize product quality. Our Research and Development Team ensures leading edge product.

YouTube Charlie Tiger Company 11 InfBat Air Assault GGJ

Footage from Dutch soldiers (Luchtmobiele Brigade/Air Assault) working in southern province Helmand, Afghanistan.

Tiger's company makes it tough. Jim Gehrz, Star Tribune. There was a little time to think as *Tiger* Woods and Vijay Singh waited ...

Tiger Force

Tiger Force was a **task force** of the **United States Army**, 1st Battalion (Airborne), 327th Infantry Regiment, 1st Brigade (Separate), **101st Airborne Division**, which fought in the **Vietnam War**.[1]

The platoon-sized unit, approximately 45 **paratroopers** was founded by Colonel **David Hackworth** in November 1965 to "outguerrilla the guerrillas."[2] Tiger Force was a highly decorated unit, and paid for its reputation with heavy casualties.[3] In October 1968, Tiger Force's parent battalion was awarded the **Presidential Unit Citation** by President **Lyndon B. Johnson**, which included a mention of Tiger Force's service at **Dak To** in June 1966.[4]

In October 2003, the **Toledo Blade** reported on members of the Tiger Force unit who had committed numerous **war crimes**—accused of killing, raping, and mutilating large numbers of noncombatant women and children.[5]

One file in these records referred to a previously unpublished war crimes investigation known as the Coy Allegation.

The statements, from both individuals who allegedly participated in the war crimes and those that did not, described war crimes such as the following:

- the routine torture and execution of prisoners[8]

- the routine practice of intentionally killing unarmed Vietnamese villagers including men, women, children, and elderly people[9]

- the routine practice of cutting off and collecting the ears of victims[10]

- the practice of wearing necklaces composed of human ears[11]

- the practice of cutting off and collecting the scalps of victims[12]

- an incident where a young mother was drugged, raped, and then executed[13]

- an incident where a soldier killed a baby and cut off his or her head after the baby's mother was killed[14]

The investigators concluded that many of the war crimes indeed took place.[15] Despite this, the Army decided not to pursue any prosecutions.[16]

Sam Ybarra sat in the darkness of his mother's Arizona home, sobbing.

Once a feared member of Tiger Force who boasted of shooting civilians, he was now a broken figure - haunted by images of the war.

"I would ask him: `What's wrong? Why are you crying?'" recalled Therlene Ramos. "He would say: `It's my life. What I did. What I did. I killed people, mama. I killed regular people. I shouldn't have. My God, what did I do?'"

Of the 30 war-crime allegations against Tiger Force investigated by the Army, Ybarra is named in seven, including the rape and fatal stabbing of a 13-year-old girl and the brutal killing of a 15-year-old boy.

Over and over, he was seen cutting off the ears of dead enemy soldiers and villagers, at times, scalping them with a hunting knife, soldiers told investigators.

Thirteen former platoon members said they were struck by the same image: Ybarra wearing necklaces of human ears.

By the time the investigation was under way in 1971, he was discharged and living on the San Carlos Apache Reservation in Arizona where he was raised. After years of alcohol and drugs, he died of pneumonia at 36.

The case reached the highest levels of the Pentagon and the Nixon White House.

Investigators concluded that 18 soldiers committed war crimes ranging from murder and assault to dereliction of duty. But no one was charged.

most war-crime cases focused on a single event, like the My Lai massacre.
The Tiger Force case is different. The atrocities took place over seven months, leaving an untold number dead - possibly several hundred civilians, former soldiers and villagers now say.

"We resorted ... to waterboarding, which is the source of much of the controversy, with only three individuals. In those cases, it was only after we'd gone through all the other steps of the process," he said on the show. "The way the whole program was set up was very careful, to use other methods and only to resort to the enhanced techniques in those special circumstances."

The memos released last month outlining the harsh interrogation methods stated that Mohammed was waterboarded 183 times and Zubaydah underwent the procedure about 83 times.

Records show that the Inquisition used three methods of torture: The prisoner could be hung by his wrists from a pulley, repeatedly hoisted and dropped. He could be tied to a rack and stretched.

Or he could be waterboarded.

Waterboarding was used in medieval times and was used by the Inquisition for more than 350 years -- from about 1478 to 1834 -- both in Spain and Mexico.

"He was tied down on a rack. His mouth was kept forcibly open and a toca or linen cloth was put down his throat to conduct water poured slowly from a jar. The severity of the torture varied with the number of jars of water used."

The Inquisition used torture in about 20 percent of the cases, Gitlitz told me. It was not used more often because even in those times "there was debate about whether testimony elicited under duress was credible," Gitlitz said.

More modern records, presumably available to Bush and Mukasey, would describe the findings of the U.S. military commission that prosecuted Japanese soldiers for waterboarding American prisoners during World War II, according to Human Rights Watch.

In 1968, A U.S. soldier was court-martialed for waterboarding a Vietnamese prisoner.

"The Bush administration continues to astonish," said Larry Cox, executive director of Amnesty International.

Cox noted that the State Department has called waterboarding torture when other countries do it, "yet in President Bush's legal wonderland, waterboarding is renamed 'an enhanced interrogation technique.'"

Bush won't say if he thinks waterboarding is torture.

"I don't want to talk about techniques," he said.

September 8, 2009

*

where do we find ourselves

out the window

out the window the big turbocharged pinon tree, old friend, waves only a
     little in the slow breeze again
its green almost yellow, drought or the beautiful light
earlier driving to the high school intense dark blue paint or chemical can in
     the back of the pickup in front
set the paler sky off through the truck slats, making it creamy and soft
Suzuki said sometimes you can't see how bright the moon is till you set it
     against the dark sky
you can get up after a so so zazen and suddenly the world appears, also the
     zazen appears
remember to thank the truck (Bill wd have put in the cart)
I lost it. perhaps it wasn't Suzuki but Eido Roshi?
wind lifts & the yellow pinon needles glint starfish or hedgehog but the sky
     bathes an intenser blue now than the gouache peeking through the
     truck slats
looming up through Tiger Force lurking back there it grows very bright
like need demand and desire it never makes sense
what's subtracted from what leaving what
could be Tiger Force suddenly searing through the pinon the sky pale
     behind it leeching out
"sometimes the world has to break open your heart so it can fill it with
     moonlight"
cried two straight days all the Tiger Force stuff strewn all over the world
     disjecta membra the nymphs' scattered limbs then her heart filled
     with moonlight
dear X   the reincarnation koan the same thing as Uji?   dear Norman rsvp
dream with the landscape
reincarnated trees just loafing, dozing
lazy in hazy light

jumpcut self-delighting mischief my daughter bangs the plate glass sliding
      door
hard birds pecking seeds I dropped scatter
do elegant rudder wing glide, taxi in for a landing a little bit down the tarmac
      & tweeze more seeds
I pick about the gravel
doves are thugs   still no difficulty has entered
snow melt comes down the mountain in spring the lizard skin wash gets
      dumped with waterfalls and the kids wade up to the waist   dogs
      caterwaul
Uji never mind
seventeen year old Y is learning to drive edging around the northern loop
      sometimes just brushing the palo verde needles a tiny bit it won't
      cost too many points
the teenagers generally grouse like professionals
grups shout their barbaric yawps over the roofs of the world
and Maggie's patrolling the yard at the end of another book
big snakes navigate the roads trying not to get extruded like Play-Doh
but one big rotting Gila Monster turns black
turkey vulture lifts off heavy and slow like a troop carrier done snacking on
      this morning's poor rabbit
and I miss my rabbit, all twenty cat intimidating pounds of him
and cat given lion cut and anesthetized tooth extraction to boot   dead too
      now
"bedraggled and happy mews at me, I'm the dream in the mirror he's trying
      to roist, or is it roust I guess, or rouse--"

which is it Fred?
I'm the cat he says in cat

today flows into today

yes the world is all that is the case
now I can say that

September 9-October 19, 2009

*

Layman Pang was leaving Yaoshan's temple, and Yaoshan ordered ten of his monks to see him off at the gate. Pang pointed to the snow falling through the air and said, "Beautiful snowflakes! They don't fall in that other place."

*

Once Layman Pang and his daughter Lingzhao were out selling bamboo baskets. Coming down off a bridge, he stumbled and fell. When Lingzhao saw this, she ran to her father and threw herself down next to him.

"What are you doing?" cried the Layman.

"I saw you fall, so I'm helping," replied Lingzhao.

"Luckily no one was looking," remarked the Layman.

September 22, 2009

ABOUT THE AUTHOR

Tenney Nathanson teaches American poetry and, from time to time, creative writing in the English Department at the University of Arizona in Tucson, where he currently directs the PhD program in literature. In 1996 he helped found the Tucson poetry and arts collective POG, which presents readings, workshops, and artists' talks. In 2008 he co-founded Tucson's Desert Rain Zen Group, affiliated with the Santa Fe based Open Source Zen project and part of the Pacific Zen School. His earlier books of poetry include *Erased Art* from Chax Press and *Home on the Range (The Night Sky with Stars in My Mouth)* from O Books. He has also published a study of Walt Whitman, *Whitman's Presence*, with New York University Press. He lives with his family in Tucson.

About Chax Press

Chax Press was founded in 1984 as a creator of handmade fine arts editions of literature, often with an inventive and playful sense of how the book arts might interact with innovative writing. Beginning in 1990 the press started to publish works in trade paperback editions, such as the current book. We currently occupy studio space, shared with the painter Cynthia Miller, in the Small Planet Bakery building at the north side of downtown Tucson, Arizona. Recent and forthcoming books by Alice Notley, Barbara Henning, Charles Bernstein, Anne Waldman, Linh Dinh, Mark Weiss, Will Alexander, and many more, may be found on our web site at chax.org.

Chax Press projects are supported by the Tucson Pima Arts Council, by the Arizona Commission on the Arts (with funding from the State of Arizona and the National Endowment for the Arts), by The Southwestern Foundation, and by many individual donors who keep us at work at the edges of contemporary literature through their generosity, friendship, and good spirits.

This book is set in Giambatista Bodoni's eponymous typeface in 11 point size. Composition and design in Adobe InDesign.